# 21 Day Mindfulness Challenge

Gill Hasson

# 21 Day Mindfulness Challenge

### Learn to live in the moment

Gill Hasson

JOHN
MURRAY
LEARNING

First published in Great Britain by John Murray Learning in 2022
An imprint of John Murray Press
A division of Hodder & Stoughton Ltd,
An Hachette UK company

1

A CIP catalogue record for this title is available from the British Library

Trade Paperback ISBN 978 1 399 80301 4

eBook ISBN 978 1 399 80303 8

Typeset by KnowledgeWorks Global Ltd.

Printed and bound in Great Britain by Clays Ltd, Elcograf S.p.A.

John Murray Press policy is to use papers that are natural, renewable and recyclable products
and made from wood grown in sustainable forests. The logging and manufacturing processes
are expected to conform to the environmental regulations of the country of origin.

John Murray Press
Carmelite House
50 Victoria Embankment
London EC4Y 0DZ

www.johnmurraypress.co.uk

# Contents

Introduction                                                    vii

Day 1: Focused meditation                                         1
Day 2: Open monitoring meditation                                 9
Day 3: Mindful awareness                                         19
Day 4: Mindful acceptance                                        27
Day 5: Self acceptance                                           39
Day 6: Accepting emotions                                        49
Day 7: Accepting others                                          59
Day 8: Mindful compassion                                        69
Day 9: Mindful forgiveness                                       79
Day 10: Letting go                                               89
Day 11: Understanding that all things pass                       99
Day 12: Beginner's mind                                         109
Day 13: Beginner's mind                                         117
Day 14: Understanding emotions                                  127
Day 15: Mindful focus                                           137
Day 16: Slowing down                                            145
Day 17: Moments of awe                                          153
Day 18: Small pleasures                                         163
Day 19: Flow                                                    173
Day 20: Mindful patience                                        181
Day 21: A mindful practice                                      191

# Introduction

## What is mindfulness?

Mindfulness is thinking about what you're doing while you're doing it. Sounds simple enough, doesn't it? But too often our minds get caught up in thoughts about the past and the future, replaying difficult situations and events from the past and imagining worst-case scenarios about the future. We're in one place doing one thing but we're thinking about the things we're not doing and the places we're not at.

It's easy to get pulled back to past events and pushed into future possibilities. You can end up living in your head – caught up in your thoughts – without realizing how those thoughts are affecting how you feel and what you do and don't do.

So how can mindfulness help? Mindfulness can help you stay grounded and feel less pushed around by what is and is not happening. A mindful approach enables you to stay focused and engaged with what you are doing and what's happening at any one time.

Mindfulness is a way to look after your mind. It teaches you how to manage distressing thoughts and difficult emotions. When you are mindful, you are better able to accept situations, yourself and other people.

### Why 21 days?

Although mindfulness is easy to learn, there are several aspects of mindfulness that require practice. Awareness and acknowledgement, acceptance, non-judgement, detachment and letting go, beginner's mind, patience and trust – these are all aspects of mindfulness that you'll learn over the next 21 days.

You'll be introduced to mindful ideas and concepts, new ways of thinking and doing. Each day builds on the previous one. As you progress through the next 21 days, you will see how the different aspects of mindfulness link together, and how they relate to and inform each other.

One day at a time, you will learn mindful ways to think and behave. Then, after 21 days, you'll have established a strong understanding and practice of mindfulness. And *because* you've spent 21 days practising mindfulness, you've already started a new habit.

Although mindfulness can become the way you approach and live your life from now on, as with any new way of thinking or doing, if it is going to become second nature it requires regular practice. It's the regular practice that strengthens any new habit.

Mindfulness is like kindness. Every day, one way or another, there are opportunities to be mindful. You don't need any special equipment or circumstances. As the author and meditation teacher Sharon Salzberg says in her book *Real Happiness: The Power of Meditation: A 28-Day Program*, 'Mindfulness is the ultimate mobile device; you can use it anywhere, anytime, unobtrusively.'

While it's not essential that you practise every single day, it's a good intention to have. However, if you don't practise mindfulness on any one day, there's no need to give up or berate yourself; that would be contrary to everything that mindfulness is all about.

Mindfulness is not a quick-fix solution for anything; it's an approach to life that, when practised with commitment and patience, can help make so many aspects of your life easier, less stressful and more enjoyable.

## How to use this book

Each of the 21 days starts with an aim and a thought for the day. Each day ends with key points and an invitation to set yourself an intention for that day.

There's plenty of explanations, ideas and suggestions to help you understand each aspect of mindfulness principles and concepts.

Every day there's one or more practical exercises for you to do. Some of them are written exercises, so you may want to have a notebook or journal to hand for the exercises and your reflections.

The exercises can be easily shared and discussed with others. In fact, you may like to go through the 21 days with one or more other people (a friend, colleague or family member). If you belong to a book club, you could suggest *21 Day Mindfulness Challenge* as a book for you all to read one month. There will certainly be plenty for you to share and discuss at your next meeting!

Whether you work through *21 Day Mindfulness Challenge* on your own or with others, begin each day with an open mind; be open to the ideas and suggestions and the exercises you are encouraged to do.

# Day 1

## AIM
To learn a simple focused meditation.

## THOUGHT FOR TODAY
*Conscious breathing is our anchor. It calms our mind and body and keeps us in the present moment.*

Mindfulness has to do with being in the present moment; being aware of and engaged in the present moment, being in the here and now, without your mind getting caught up in what did or didn't happen or what has or hasn't happened yet.

How can you best begin to be aware of and engaged in the present moment? By using the one phenomenon that is always with you: your breathing. Your breathing is the one thing that is always happening right here, right now and that you can choose to be aware of. An awareness of your breathing provides a focal point for your mind that can help slow everything down, calm your mind and your body and bring you into the present moment.

### Exercise: Breathe

Before you read any further, close your eyes and breathe in and then breathe out. Do this three times.

That wasn't difficult was it?

Do it again. Close your eyes and this time, breathe in, then out, five times. With each breath in, be aware of the rhythm of breathing in. And then be aware of breathing out.

You've just done a 30-second meditation.

## Simple focused-breathing meditation

Being aware of your breathing is a simple thing you can do anywhere, at any time, for as short or as long a time as you wish.

You don't need to change how you breathe or control your breath in any way. There's no need to breathe any deeper than you normally would. Simply pay attention to breathing in and out. If your mind begins to think of other things, or you get distracted by a sound or sensation, just notice it and return your attention back to your breath.

You might find yourself noticing the rhythm of breathing in and out or feel the air going in and out of your nose, or the air as it enters and leaves your lungs. But whatever you notice about your breathing, with a simple breathing meditation, you're just sitting and breathing. When you notice that your mind has wandered and is thinking about something else, just go back to being aware of your breathing.

There is no need to judge yourself if your mind wanders; once you realize you are caught in thinking, simply let the thoughts go and return your attention back to your breath each time. Bring it back to the breath, again and again. You're not sitting there with a blank mind, you are simply breathing and bringing the focus back to your breathing.

That's it. That's all. It's a simple mindful focused-breathing meditation.

## Popular misconception

You may think that meditation is about clearing your mind of thoughts. Not so!

Even experienced meditators find they can't focus on their breathing for too long without thoughts coming into their minds. Your mind *will* wander to thoughts about other things. And that's ok.

Memories from the past, personal problems, problems of the world, worries and hopes for the future will come into your mind and distract you. This is normal. With a simple focused-breathing meditation, there's nothing to do but to calmly bring your mind back to the present, to your breathing, each and every time.

### Exercise: The pink flamingo

Imagine a pink flamingo.

Now close your eyes and focus on your breathing. Do this for about one minute.

*Do not think about the pink flamingo!*

Not easy was it? An image of the pink flamingo probably kept coming back into your mind. But each time, all you had to do was bring your mind back to your breathing.

# Letting thoughts pass

It's only natural that thoughts will come into your head and, if given attention, take you out of the present moment. With mindful meditation, you learn to be aware of thoughts, feelings and emotions that arise in your mind and you then let them pass like clouds floating across the sky or leaves floating down a stream.

Just know that each time you come back to your breathing, you are bringing your attention to the present moment. So the practice isn't actually sitting there with a blank mind; it's simply breathing and bringing the focus back to your breathing. Beginning again each and every time is the actual practice, not a problem to be overcome so that one day you can come to the 'real' meditation.

Each time you are aware that your mind has wandered and you calmly bring your focus back to your breathing, you'll be a little more experienced at letting thoughts go and engaging with the present moment.

## THE SCIENCE

A study published in 2021 in the journal *Scientific Reports* showed that daily meditation for just ten minutes a day causes 'marked changes' in the ability to return to focused concentration in other situations, when for example, you are working and get interrupted or distracted.

Researchers at Binghamton University, New York, taught students how to meditate, and then asked them to practise meditating for five days a week for eight weeks. MRI brain scans were taken before and after the students started meditating.

'The findings indicate the potential effects of meditation on enhancing the brain capability of fast switching between mind wandering and focused attention and maintaining attention once in attentive states,' the study concluded. In other words, a mindful breathing meditation helps train and strengthen your ability to bring your mind back to what's happening and what you're doing in the present.

# The benefits of a regular meditation practice

A daily meditation practice, in a wide range of everyday situations, means you will be able to more easily return your attention to the present. This can be beneficial in a number of ways. When, for example you're engaged in an activity, task or piece of work, and your mind gets distracted or interrupted, mindfulness brings you back to what you are doing. (More about this on Day 15.)

But that's not all. If, as you go about your day, your mind gets stuck in the past – ruminating, regretting, resenting or feeling guilty about something that happened yesterday, last week, last year or years ago – regular mindful meditation practice will make it more likely that you will be aware that your mind is unhelpfully stuck thinking about those past events and you will then bring yourself back to the present. (More about this on Day 14.)

And, when you are worried or anxious, regular mindful meditation practices help make it more likely that you will be aware that your mind has leapt ahead to the future – to what may or may not happen – and you will bring yourself back to the present.

A mindful meditation practice trains your mind to be less reactive to stressful events. Whatever else is or isn't happening within you, for you or around you, mindful breathing meditations provide an anchor, helping you feel calm, balanced and grounded.

Mindful breathing meditation is like a reset button that you can push to return yourself to the present moment whenever you feel the need. It is an effective way of orienting yourself to the now, not because the breath has some magical property, but because it's always there with you.

Quite simply, a regular, daily meditation practice helps you to be mindful in all you do and experience.

## Meditation with a mantra or visual focus

'When you own your breath, nobody can steal your peace.'

Author unknown

With a simple focused-attention meditation, you focus on your breath to focus your mind to the present. And when your mind wanders, you bring it back to the breath, again and again.

To avoid being discouraged by the fact that thoughts *will* come into your head, focusing on an object, a word, or a phrase can be helpful. A common practice is to focus your gaze on the flame of a candle or anything that you find visually engaging – a lava lamp or a screensaver moving image such as 'Blue glitter particles' which you can search for on YouTube. You can find more images similar to this by Googling 'relaxing screensaver'.

Maintaining your gaze on a moving image, a still image or an object can help develop your ability to remain focused in the present. You might, though, find it more helpful to synchronize your breathing with a simple mantra. Mantras are effective in helping maintain your awareness as you breathe in and breathe out. A mantra focuses on one thought, word or phrase. It is something you can say to yourself during meditation that helps avoid other thoughts coming into your mind because it is already engaged with one single thought.

All you need to do is to establish steady, even breathing. There's no need for your mind to control the pace of the breath. Simply allow the breath, its evenness and depth, to still the pace of your mind. And then, in time with your breathing, say a mantra. You can say it out loud or in your head.

### Try it now

Here are four examples of mantras:

- Breathing in: '*I am breathing in.*' Breathing out: '*I am breathing out.*'
- Breathing in: '*I breathe in calm.*' Breathing out: '*I breathe out stillness and peace.*'
- Breathing in: '*Calm.*' Breathing out: '*Peace.*'
- Breathing in: '*I am here.*' Breathing out: '*I am present.*'

Mantras are personal. They are a positive phrase or affirmation that you choose or make up for yourself, which resonates with you. If you find that a mantra works for you, but at some point, you get bored with the mantra you have chosen, simply change it for a different one.

DAY 1

# One minute counts

Dan Harris, co-anchor of US television's *ABC News Nightline* and the weekend edition of *Good Morning America* learned to meditate after having a panic attack on live television a few years ago. In an interview with online magazine *Forbes* in November 2020, Harris, the author of *10% Happier*, explained that meditation doesn't require a massive time commitment. 'I tell people one minute counts. I'd rather see people do five to ten minutes a day, but I'm quite familiar with the diabolical difficulty of habit formation. So I like to use two little slogans: "one minute counts" and "daily-ish." If you can set a loose goal and have a sense of experimentation and humour ... as you establish a habit, I think it's possible.'

---

### Exercise: Start a habit

Today, set a gentle alarm – a mindfulness bell – on your phone for four different times during the day. Each time the bell rings, stop what you are doing and do one minute of focused breathing.

In your journal, you may want to write about how you felt doing a focused meditation. What feelings came up? Peace and calm? Frustration, irritation, impatience?

---

# Key points

- With a simple focused-breathing meditation, you simply pay attention to your breathing. When you notice that your mind is thinking about something else, there's no need to judge yourself or to feel annoyed or impatient. Just return your attention back to your breath each and every time.

- You may find that a visual focus or a mantra helps you to maintain focus during meditation.

- A regular meditation practice is inherently calming and grounding. It also trains your mind so that in everyday situations, if you are interrupted or distracted, you can return your focus to whatever it is you are doing. You will be more aware of when you are overly caught up in regrets, concerns or worries. You can let go and stay in the here and now.

- **Set yourself an intention:** at the end of today, commit to doing a focused meditation every day for the next 20 days. Choose a time of day – it could be the morning, maybe lunchtime, mid-afternoon, on the train home from work, or in the evening. Decide a realistic length of time that you will meditate for – it could be for one minute, two minutes, five minutes or more.

# Day 2

## AIM

To recognize that your thoughts are separate from you.

## THOUGHT FOR TODAY

*Thoughts are just thoughts. We can be the observer of our thoughts, we don't have to be the thoughts themselves.*

Yesterday you learned a simple focused-attention meditation. As you focused on your breathing, when you were aware that a thought had come into your head, you were encouraged to simply return your attention to your breath.

Just as experienced meditators find they can't focus on their breathing for too long without thoughts coming into their minds, you'll find that your mind will wander too. And that's ok. Thinking is normal. Like everyone else, you're human. Thinking is what we do.

---

### Exercise: An 'open monitoring' meditation

Start today with a one-minute focused-breathing meditation. Just as you did yesterday, focus on your breathing. When you are aware that a thought has come into your head, return your attention back to your breath.

Today, you are going to learn an 'open monitoring' meditation.

- As with a focused-attention meditation, focus your attention on breathing in and breathing out.
- This time though, when you notice that a thought has come into your mind, before you go back to focusing on your breathing, *acknowledge* the thought. Tell yourself: 'A thought has come into my mind.' Then return your attention back to your breathing.
- That's it. It's that simple.

So for example, if you had a thought 'I must remember to phone my friend', you acknowledge that thought by saying to yourself, 'I've just had a thought that I need to remember to phone my friend.'

---

## What's the point?

What, you might ask, is the point of that? Why would I want to be aware of and acknowledge my thoughts?

As human beings, our ability to think is amazing. As well as being capable of thinking about things that *are* happening, we can think about:

- things that did and didn't happen
- things that have happened
- things that might happen
- things that may never happen at all.

We can plan and anticipate good things, remember happy times, reminisce, analyse, rationalize and reason. But our ability to think in these ways is not always a blessing. Sometimes, our minds ruminate and we get trapped thinking back over difficult and distressing events and experiences. As well as uncomfortable thoughts about past events, our minds can get caught up in distressing thoughts about the future, worrying and anxious thoughts about events that may or may not happen. Other times our mind may be racing; jumping from one thing to the next, often unrelated thing. It appears that our mind has a life of its own and we just can't switch it off.

Feeling overwhelmed by our thoughts, getting caught up in thoughts about the past or the future, takes us away from living now, in the present. When you're at work, for example, you may be thinking about being on holiday; then when you are on holiday, you're worrying about work.

A mindful approach suggests that you don't have to get caught up in upsetting, stressful or distressing thoughts. You don't have to believe what your thoughts tell you or react to them in any way. Mindfulness recognizes thoughts for what they are: mental events.

---

## Exercise: Recognize thoughts

Over the next few days, be aware of the first three thoughts you have upon waking every day. Write them down in your journal. Were they ordinary neutral thoughts, positive thoughts or were they judgmental, anxious, apprehensive or blaming?

For example, on waking up, a neutral thought could be: 'Time to get up.' A positive thought could be: 'Oh good, time to get up – I'm looking forward to today.' And a negative unhelpful thought could be: 'Oh God. Time to get up. Already. I'm not looking forward to today.'

# Creating a space between yourself and your thoughts

It's not easy to take a step back from your thoughts and create a space that allows you to see your thoughts for what they are: mental events. But, the good news is that practising an 'open monitoring' meditation trains your mind and helps you to step back and 'see' your thoughts more easily.

Just as physical exercise strengthens your body, meditation is a mental exercise that strengthens your mind.

The more you practise 'open monitoring' meditation, the better your ability to acknowledge your thoughts as separate from you will be. And the more you are able to acknowledge thoughts as separate from you, the easier it will be for you, in your everyday life, to notice when your thoughts are taking over and to realize that your thoughts are simply 'mental events'. You know that there's no need for you to identify with your thoughts, attach yourself to them, believe them or be distressed by them in any way. Your thoughts do not have to control you.

Mindfulness doesn't stop with meditation. It helps inform and guide all aspects of our lives. With an 'open monitoring' meditation practice we can shift our relationship to ourselves and our thoughts and feelings in a way that allows for greater perspective and understanding.

Pausing to acknowledge and observe your thoughts creates a space between how and what you think, and how you respond to those thoughts. That space can help you better respond to your thoughts instead of automatically believing them, reacting to them, and getting overwhelmed or stuck in them.

## Thinking about your own thinking

Thinking about your own thinking is a process known as 'metacognition'. This is derived from the Greek word *meta*, meaning 'beyond' or 'after'. Metacognition involves taking a step beyond yourself and your thoughts so that you can look back at and try to understand them.

Psychologists call this ability to step back from your thoughts, 'cognitive defusion'. When you believe and get caught up in unhelpful thoughts, you are 'fusing' with your thoughts. Ordinarily, when something is fused, it unites or blends into a whole, as if melting together. So, when you fuse with your thoughts, it's as if you are your thoughts and you have become one entity.

However, when something 'defuses', it becomes weaker. So, with cognitive defusion, you are looking *at* thoughts rather than *being* them. And this weakens the link between you and your thoughts. You recognize them for what they are – separate from you.

Here are some examples.

In a situation that you may have been anxious about, you may have had the thought:

'I'm not going to cope. They'll think I'm hopeless.'

Or you may have had the thought about someone else:

'My friend hasn't been in contact for quite some time now. He obviously doesn't care about me.'

Or, concerning something you've recently done, you might think:

'I've made a mistake. I can never do anything right.'

You have one of these thoughts and you believe the thought to be true; that you are '*not* going to cope', for example, or that your 'friend *doesn't* care' or that you can '*never* do anything right'. You have 'fused' with your thought.

If you step back from any one of those thoughts – if you 'defuse' from any of them – you can tell yourself:

'This is simply a thought I'm having. I'm just telling myself this.'

You are aware of the thoughts as thoughts and not necessarily as being true or reflecting reality.

## Try it now

Think about something you are worried or anxious about. It might be, for example, 'I'm going to fail the exam.'

> Whatever your concern or worrying thought, now tell yourself: 'Here's the thought that ...' So in this example, you would tell yourself 'Here's the thought that I might fail that exam.'
>
> By practising 'open monitoring' meditation practice, rather than getting caught up in your thoughts, you are able to create a space in your mind that separates you from your thoughts. You can then gain a perspective that helps you to see and understand things differently in a way that is calming and reassuring.

## Metaphors to help you with cognitive defusion

On Day 1, you learned that with a focused meditation you become aware of the thoughts that arise in your mind and you simply return your attention back to your breathing.

An 'open monitoring' meditation is a step on from a focused meditation. With an 'open monitoring' meditation you practise being aware of your thoughts, but before they pass, you acknowledge the thoughts that arise in your mind as just thoughts, and *then* let them pass. You acknowledge your thoughts and you allow your mind to move on without losing your awareness of the present.

To help you create some distance from your thoughts – to acknowledge your thoughts but not engage with them – you may find it helpful to imagine your thoughts as being like one of the following:

- Trains coming and going while you stand watching from the platform. You don't have to get on board.
- Buses coming and going but you don't have to get on them and be taken away.
- Guests entering a hotel. You can be like the doorman: you greet the guests but you don't follow them to their rooms.
- Suitcases dropping onto a conveyor belt at the airport. You can watch them pass by, without having to pick them up.

- People passing by you in the street. You can nod your head at them, but you don't have to stop and have a conversation.
- Actors on a stage. You can watch the play, but you don't need to get on stage and perform.
- Junk email. You can't stop it from coming in, but you don't have to read it!

## Breathe

Once you have acknowledged a thought, you may find it helpful, with your breathing, to let the thought go when you exhale. Each time you breathe out, you let go and release your thoughts about the past and future. Then as you inhale you bring your attention back to your breath and your awareness is restored. The breath acts as your anchor to the present moment.

## Mindful meditation – 'a new way of being'

Journalist Jon Wilde spent many years interviewing rock stars and A-list celebrities for national newspapers and magazines. However, towards the end of 2012 Jon's life took a turn – health problems, financial problems and drinking too much all added up to what Jon describes as 'quicksands of disquiet on all sides'.

Then he discovered mindfulness.

On the Everyday Mindfulness website (www.everyday-mindfulness. org) Jon writes: 'In meditation, I discovered the kind of quiet spaciousness that I'd been looking for all my life. With practice, I learned how to carry that quiet spaciousness away from the meditation bench and into the rest of my day. Truly, it felt like I had found an entirely new way of being. It felt like I had finally come home to myself in a meaningful way.'

## Exercise: Observing your thoughts

This exercise can help you recognize thoughts as separate from yourself. You simply need to put aside five minutes for an 'open monitoring' meditation.

- Begin the meditation. As you focus on your breathing, each time a thought arises, pause and write it down. Whatever the thought, write it down. Then return to your breathing.
- Don't try to have thoughts, but at the same time, try not to suppress your thoughts. Just focus on your breathing. Each and every time a thought arises, write it down.
- At the end of the meditation, look at the words you have written down. You are literally observing your thoughts. How good to know that you *can* be the observer of your thoughts and not the thoughts themselves!

When you start meditating it often seems like you're having more thoughts than ever. That's not a bad thing! It's an indication that you are more aware of your thoughts; aware of them as separate entities. Don't be discouraged. Just acknowledge their presence and let them come and go without pursuing them further.

# Affirmations

Choose one of these affirmations to say to yourself to help remind you that your thoughts are separate from you:

- Thoughts are just thoughts.
- I am not my thoughts.
- I can step back from my thoughts.
- I don't have to believe the negative thoughts I tell myself.

# Key points

- With an 'open monitoring' meditation, you focus your attention on breathing in and breathing out. When you notice that a thought has come into your mind, before you go back to focusing on your breathing, acknowledge the thought.

- Practising an 'open monitoring' meditation trains your mind to step back and 'see' your thoughts more easily. You are in a position to understand them as separate entities. You realize that thoughts are just thoughts. You don't have to believe what your thoughts tell you or react to them in any way.

- **Set yourself an intention**: at the end of today, commit to doing an 'open monitoring' meditation every day for the next 20 days. Choose a time of day – it could be the morning, maybe lunchtime, mid-afternoon, on the train home from work, or in the evening. Decide on a realistic length of time that you will meditate for – it could be for one minute, two minutes, five minutes or more. Just practise focusing on your breathing, acknowledging then letting go of your thoughts.

# Day 3

## AIM
To be more aware of what's happening in the world around you.

## THOUGHT FOR TODAY
*'When you reach the end of what you should know, you will be at the beginning of what you should sense.'*

*Kahlil Gibrán*

Mindful breathing meditations encourage you to be aware of and acknowledge your breathing and your thoughts – what's happening within you. Mindful awareness and acknowledgement is also practised by being open and receptive to what's happening in the world around you.

## Try it now

Listen. Stop reading right now and listen for one minute. Close your eyes and listen to the sounds inside – your breathing, a ticking clock, children moving around, other people talking, the TV or radio. Or maybe just silence. As well as the sounds inside, be aware of the sounds outside – traffic, people, birds, the wind or rain. Or again, the silence.

From now on, each morning when you wake up, lie for a minute or two being aware of and acknowledging the sounds that you hear.

## Exercise: The five senses meditation

Your hearing isn't, of course, the only sense you have. You have five senses. As well as sound, you have sight, smell, taste and touch. The five senses meditation involves a simple sequence of steps that requires you to notice what you are experiencing with each of your five senses; to be aware of what is happening right here, right now.

Today, you may want to write down each of the things that your five senses experience during this exercise, but in future, you can simply do the exercise without noting them down.

- **Notice five things that you can see:** Look for things that you may not normally notice, something tiny for example, or something up high. Notice shadows, colours, shapes and patterns.

- **Notice four things that you can feel:** Next, bring your awareness to four things that you can feel. Feel your feet in your shoes for example. Notice the texture – the smooth surface of a table you are resting your hands on, the softness of a piece of clothing, a blanket, or a towel. Notice the feel of it in your hands or against your face. Feel the warmth or the coldness of something.
- **Notice three things you can hear:** As in the 'Try it now' exercise above, take a minute or two to listen and note three things that you hear. Notice sounds that you might not otherwise have paid attention to – the hum of the refrigerator, your breathing, a ticking clock, children moving around, other people talking, the TV or radio. Make your own sounds – slowly slide your feet along the floor, rub your hands along a surface, click your fingers. Or just allow silence. Be aware of the sounds outside – traffic, people, birds, the wind or rain. Or again, the silence.
- **Notice two things you can smell:** Bring your awareness to smells around you – the air that you breathe, the smell of your clothes or your hands.
- **Notice one thing you can taste:** Focus on one thing that you can taste right now, at this moment. Notice the taste in your mouth. Drink or eat something – something that has a distinct flavour like a mint sweet or a slice of lemon, or a very subtle flavour like water. Or just open your mouth, suck in the air and taste it.

## Five senses meditation for grounding

The five senses meditation can train your mind to be more aware of everyday occurrences – the sights, sounds, smells and tastes of the present moment – and help to interrupt the autopilot mode you are in so often during your day. You can gain new perspectives and appreciation for the ordinary things and events in the world around you.

But that's not all. With the five senses meditation, everything that you notice happens in the moment. Being present in this way – because you are aware of what's actually taking place right here right now – whenever things feel off-balance and out of your control, the five senses meditation can connect you directly and immediately with the present moment, allowing you to feel grounded; mentally and emotionally calm and stable; balanced and centred. Rather than getting caught up in or overwhelmed by thoughts and feelings, you are engaged with what's right here, right now *outside* your head.

As well as raising your awareness and helping you to feel grounded, being more aware of the sights, sounds, smells, feelings and tastes occurring in the moment also allows for greater access to your intuition.

## Tuning in to your intuition

Intuition is that keen and quick insight, that immediate knowing, that tells you something is or isn't happening – that it is or isn't 'right'. Everyone has intuition; it bridges the gap between the conscious and non-conscious parts of your mind, between instinct and reason.

Tuning in to your intuition simply means being aware, at any one time, of the information that one or more of your senses are communicating to you: what your ears, eyes, nose, sense of taste sense of touch and the physical sensations are telling you at any one moment.

Intuition happens in the present. Intuitive messages are brief and quick which makes them easy to miss. Not only that, but intuitive messages are often drowned out by internal and external noise and activity that may be happening in and around you.

Mindfulness can though, help you to filter out mental chatter and external noise, activity and distractions, and to focus.

### Exercise: Practise developing your intuition

- Notice what's normal *and* what's new and different in familiar situations. Take a couple of minutes to be still and be present in a range of situations at home, on your way to work, at work, in a café, and so on.
- What do you see or hear, smell, taste, touch and feel? By being more aware of what your senses tell you is normal, when you notice things being out of place or unusual you will recognize your intuition communicating with you.

- Tune in to your intuition. Learn to trust your hunches and gut feelings. If something doesn't look, sound, taste, smell or feel right, focus. Don't allow anything else to divert your attention.
- Listen to your body. In any one situation an inkling or flash of inner sense might be felt as a tightness in your chest, a lump in your throat, lightness in your head, a voice, or a sensation, even a taste.
- Be alert for a combination of signals; it might be a glimpse of something happening; a movement *and* a momentary sound. When all the information your senses are receiving does add up, your intuition is coming through loud and clear!

## Making meditation a habit

Whether you practise a focused meditation, an 'open monitoring' meditation, the five senses meditation or any other meditation – they all take practice.

It's like exercise. If you are hoping to run a marathon, you run short distances to begin with and build up to running the full distance. And if you want to strengthen your body at the gym, at first, you may struggle with small weights and feel that you will never manage the larger weights. But with regular practice, your muscles become stronger and you progress to heavier weights and resistance exercises.

Just as regular physical exercise develops physical ability and strength and leads to a fit, healthy body, regular meditation is the mental exercise that develops mindfulness and leads to increased focus, engagement, balance and calm in your everyday life.

It's the regular practice that is key. How come? Well, when you think or do something in a new way, you create new connections, or 'neural pathways' in your brain. Then, every time you repeat that thought or action, every time you continue using these new pathways, they become stronger and more established.

It's like walking through a field of long grass – each step helps to create a new path and every time you walk that new path you establish a clear route which becomes easier to use each time. It becomes a habit to use that route.

By setting yourself an intention to make meditation a daily practice, in time, you will see your ability to meditate develop, and the positive effects increase. However, although you make a concerted effort to practise a mindful meditation on a daily basis, it's easy to get distracted by a myriad of things that divert your attention through the day and an intention to meditate can fall by the wayside.

So how can you make mindful meditation a habit, something that you do on a regular basis until it becomes your normal, everyday practice? Here are two suggestions:

- **Know that one minute counts**: Start with a short, doable, realistic amount of time for meditating, for example, one, two or three minutes at a time. With this approach, you train in being present, a few minutes at a time.

- **Try the 'If ... then ...' approach**: You may find it helpful to have a regular time – one that fits into your lifestyle and your commitment – to meditate each day, or you can try the '*If ... then ...*' approach. With this approach, you make meditation a habit by creating links, connecting a new habit (meditation) to an already established habit. For example, you might be in the habit of sitting down with a cup of tea when you come home from work each day. You could choose to link the activity of meditating with the habit of having a cup of tea. In this way you attach a new habit – meditating – to an already established habit – drinking tea when you come in from work. So *if* you have a cup of tea when you get home from work, *then* you'll also spend some time meditating before or after you've drunk your tea.

# Key points

- As well as being aware of your breathing and acknowledging your thoughts – what's happening within you – mindful awareness and acknowledgement is also practised by being open and receptive to what else is happening in the world outside of yourself.

- The five senses meditation involves a simple sequence of steps that requires you to notice what you are experiencing with each of your five senses; to be aware of what is happening right here, right now.

- **Set yourself an intention:** Make mindful meditation a habit. Make it easy for yourself; start with a short, doable, realistic amount of time for meditating; one, two or three minutes at a time. Have a regular time – one that fits into your lifestyle and your commitment – to meditate each day, or try the 'If ... then ...' approach, linking a new habit (meditation) to an already established habit.

# Day 4

**AIM**

To understand and practise mindful acceptance.

**THOUGHT FOR TODAY**

*'Happiness can only exist in acceptance.'*

*George Orwell*

Over the last three days, you've been introduced to mindful awareness meditation. You've learned and practised two simple meditations: a focused, attention-based meditation and an 'open monitoring' meditation. You've also learned and practised the five senses meditation. The emphasis has been on awareness and acknowledgement.

Today, you will be introduced to the concept of mindful acceptance.

---

### Exercise: Meditation

Before you read any further, start with a focused-attention meditation. Sit silently for two or three minutes and focus on your breathing. When you notice that a thought has come into your mind, simply return your attention back to your breathing.

---

## Meditation and acceptance

With a focused-attention meditation, not only are you practising mindful awareness, but you are also practising mindful acceptance. Acceptance, along with non-judgement, trust and patience, is one of the core attitudes of mindfulness. In a focused-attention meditation, you *accept* your thoughts and let them pass. You *accept* your mind has wandered and thoughts have come into your head. There's no need to judge yourself or feel disappointed or frustrated if thoughts enter your head. You simply *accept* that your mind has wandered and return your awareness to breathing. In an 'open monitoring' meditation, you practise acceptance when you accept your thoughts as separate entities; that they are just thoughts.

Of course, this is easier said than done!

When Dr. Shauna Shapiro attended her first meditation retreat in Thailand, she soon realized that she was not in control of her mind. Describing her experience in her book *Good Morning, I Love you: Mindfulness, & self compassion to rewire your brain*, Dr Shapiro says 'I would attend to one breath, two breaths, maybe three and then my mind was gone, lost in thoughts.' Frustrated and impatient, she began to wonder,

'Why can't I do this? Everyone else looks like they're sitting so peacefully. What's wrong with me?'

On her fourth day of the retreat, she met with a monk who asked her how she was doing. She replied, 'I'm a terrible meditator. I can't do it. I am trying so hard, and every time I try harder, I get even more tangled up. Meditation must be for other, more spiritual, calmer kinds of people. I don't think this is the right path for me.'

The monk looked at Shauna with compassion and a humorous twinkle in his eye. 'Oh dear, you're not practicing mindfulness,' he told her. 'You are practicing impatience, judgment, frustration, and striving.' Then he said five words that changed her life 'What you practice grows stronger.'

He explained that mindfulness is not just about focusing attention, it's about how you pay attention, with an attitude of kindness and acceptance.

Rather than get frustrated and impatient, she needed to accept that her mind had wandered during meditation and gently bring it back to the present moment with kindness.

## Understanding acceptance

Acceptance is an attitude, a state of mind. It's a way of thinking about and understanding something, yourself, someone else, an event or situation. Acceptance is the understanding that things have or haven't happened. Or that things are or are not happening right now. And that things may or may not happen in the future.

A helpful way to understand acceptance is to imagine this everyday scenario:

You lose your keys and your mobile phone. You are sure that they must be somewhere in the house, so you start searching. No luck. You try the car – perhaps they fell out of your bag and fell under the seat? They are not there. You are getting increasingly frustrated. You cannot believe you could have mislaid them. You call your partner. Have they seen your keys and mobile phone? No. You set off for work, feeling annoyed and confused.

A couple of days pass. You just cannot accept you could have lost both your keys and your phone. How? Where? Maybe they were stolen? To make matters worse, this is the second phone you've lost in the space of a few months. 'Why has this happened to me?' you ask yourself. 'It's not fair!'

The next day, you acknowledge to yourself that the phone and keys have gone. You turn your attention to what to do now. You get new keys cut and you buy a new phone.

Notice how, in this example, once you acknowledge and accept that what has happened *has* happened – that the keys and phone are gone – you can free your mind to think about what to do next, in the present.

In situations like this, getting stuck in denial, disappointment and frustration won't make things un-happen. Mindfulness encourages you to see that when you are in resistance to a given situation, you are allowing the past to dominate the present. What could be more futile than resisting what already is? This doesn't mean you can't do anything about the situation as it is now, but before you do, you need to accept what has brought you to this point; to this present moment.

## Exercise: Difficult situations

Which of these situations and events has ever happened to you?

- You didn't get something you really wanted – the job, a place on the team or on the course.
- You failed a test or an exam.
- On the phone, you were kept on hold for a long time.
- A friend let you down.
- A holiday didn't turn out well or was ruined in some way.
- You spent a lot of time or money on something that for some reason, didn't work out.
- You lost your job.
- An event you were looking forward to was cancelled.
- Someone else achieved something you wanted or did better than you.
- A friendship or relationship ended.

What do you remember about your reaction to the situations you experienced? In your journal, write down what your thoughts may have been at the time. Also, describe how often and how many days, weeks, or months you continued to relive the situation, going back over what did or didn't happen.

## SIX SIGNS THAT YOU HAVE NOT ACCEPTED A SITUATION

It's not easy to recognize that you are stuck in resentment, regret, denial, frustration or anger about a situation. Here are six signs to help you be more aware:

1. You often relive the situation, going back over what did or didn't happen.

2. When you think about what did or didn't happen, you still feel upset or angry.

3. You often wonder about what could have been.

4. You either refuse to talk about it to other people, or you keep bringing it up with other people.

5. You keep blaming yourself or whoever you think is responsible for what happened.

6. You often say to yourself: 'Why me?', 'It's not fair', 'It shouldn't be this way', 'I can't believe this has happened' or 'What *is* the matter with people?'

Of course, it's not easy to accept difficulties and problems, unwanted situations or unfairness. No one wants to experience pain, disappointment, sadness or loss. But those experiences are an inevitable part of life.

When you allow difficult emotions to overwhelm you, you add suffering to your pain. You have a choice. You can create more misery with your thoughts, or you can decrease your suffering by practising acceptance.

# Popular misconception

Acceptance doesn't mean that you have to resign yourself to something, to give in and believe you can't do anything about what has happened or is happening. Of course, life brings problems and difficulties and it's not easy to manage when you're wishing those things had never happened. But accepting what has happened means recognizing that you cannot change what has *already* happened.

With acceptance you simply acknowledge the situation and your circumstances as they actually are right now, rather than how you wish they would be or had been.

Acceptance brings a state of calm, where you can rest without necessarily needing things to be different. What happens next, what you choose to do, has to come out of your understanding of where you or the situation is right now. When you begin to accept the way things are now, rather than put up with a situation, resist it or fight it, you free your mind to move forward in positive ways.

## Being non-judgemental

Acceptance goes hand in hand with another aspect of mindfulness: non judgement. Being non-judgemental means that, rather than see something that has happened or is happening as 'good' or 'bad', 'right' or 'wrong', you just experience or observe it.

In fact, in a situation that you may already be finding challenging – meditation for example, or losing your keys and phone – when you *do* give meaning to experiences and events (when you are negative, critical and judgemental), you actually extend the suffering.

Mindfulness is about being aware of that and taking a fresh perspective. It involves noticing your experience as it is and not as your mind judges it. This approach can then open you to the possibility of understanding things in a different way.

## Radical acceptance

Being able to accept a situation and not extend the difficulties and challenges into further suffering is often referred to as 'radical acceptance'. Radical acceptance recognizes that with a difficult or unwanted situation, resisting and railing against it just makes things worse. Radical acceptance is a conscious decision to see things differently.

While you may not be able to change a situation, you can choose how you interpret it. Radical acceptance recognizes that there is always the chance to move forward in a positive, helpful way. You just have to find it.

It's important to know, however, that whether it takes a day or two to get over losing your keys and phone, or months to get over something more serious, acceptance cannot be rushed. It is part of a process that may involve feelings such as denial, refusal, opposition, fear, regret and guilt.

In the 1980s, Canadian-American actor Michael J. Fox, had a hugely successful career as a Hollywood film and TV actor. As well as appearing in the Emmy award-winning TV series *Family Ties*, Michael was the star of *Back to the Future*, one of the biggest films of the 1980s.

Then, in 1991 at the age of 30, he was diagnosed with young-onset Parkinson's disease.

Michael's initial symptoms were a twitching little finger and a sore shoulder, but he was told that his condition would become increasingly debilitating and within a few years he would no longer be able to work.

In his book *Lucky Man*, published in 2002, Michael wrote about how, after seven years of denial and depression, he eventually accepted his diagnosis, gave up drinking and went public about having Parkinson's disease. He set up The Michael J. Fox Foundation, dedicated to finding a cure for Parkinson's disease through funded research and ensuring the development of improved therapies for those living with Parkinson's today.

## Popular misconception

It's important to know that acceptance does not mean accepting the unacceptable. Any situation that leaves you or anyone else unsafe and at risk of physical or mental danger is not acceptable. Unsafe working or living conditions, for example, are unacceptable situations. An abusive relationship with a partner, family member, friend or colleague or anyone else is not acceptable. Being harassed, taken advantage of, or being treated unfairly or with disrespect, are not situations to be accepted. Experiencing mental health problems – depression, anxiety, panic attacks, burnout or suicidal feelings – none of these are acceptable.

However, it's only by accepting that one of these situations *has happened* or *is happening* that you can move forward and do something about it. Not accepting happens when you deny or ignore the problem or see the situation as unfair and not your fault and you get stuck in thinking that way. With radical acceptance, you acknowledge that it *is* unfair, unsafe, intolerable. You accept that.

You can move on but before you do, you need to accept what has brought you to this point, to this present moment. In fact, in what's known as the 'acceptance paradox', acceptance *is* what makes change possible. If you don't acknowledge and accept what has happened and what is happening, it's difficult to move on from that point. It's a strategic acceptance; you may not like what's happening, but accepting that it has happened, or is happening, you free your mind to think more clearly.

## Meditation: A place to practise acceptance

When you practise a focused-awareness meditation you also practise acceptance. As you focus on your breathing, each time a thought enters your head, rather than get frustrated, you simply accept you've lost focus and you return your attention to your breathing. And in an 'open monitoring' meditation you accept your thoughts as just thoughts.

In this way, meditation can help you develop acceptance for everyday occurrences; you train your mind to be more able to accept everyday annoyances and the more difficult challenges in life. You learn not to make a difficulty worse by railing against it.

Certainly, it's difficult to accept what you don't want to be true. But not accepting makes things more difficult because, by not accepting, you exacerbate – increase the severity – of your distress.

## Allow yourself to be sad, upset or angry

It's a natural reaction to be upset or angry when things don't turn out as you'd hoped. Accepting a situation isn't easy; you are not expected to accept everything immediately. Allow yourself to be sad, upset, angry etc., but know that holding on only holds you back from living in the present. There comes a point when you need to move on. On Day 14 you will learn more about how to move on from difficult, uncomfortable feelings.

## Exercise: Practise acceptance in everyday life

*Acceptance of what has happened is the first step to overcoming the consequences of any misfortune.*

*William James*

As well as meditation being a valuable way to practise acceptance, you can practise acceptance with the ordinary everyday irritations and annoyances in life.

Start by accepting small things, such as mislaying your keys or phone, missing the bus or train, your coffee not being hot enough, the excess plastic packaging on your groceries, the rubbish in the streets, being cut off the phone call after you've been holding on for ten minutes.

If there's something that regularly irritates or annoys you, use that as an opportunity to practise acceptance.

- Notice thoughts you have, such as 'I just can't believe it', 'It's not fair', 'I'm still so upset', 'It makes me so angry'.
- Now, tell yourself, 'It's happened. Nothing can change that. No need for me to get stuck in how unfair or ridiculous it is.'
- Give yourself an accepting affirmation, such as 'It is what it is'. Repeat the affirmation to yourself. Remind yourself that 'it is what it is'.
- Ask yourself, 'What can I do to solve the problem?' or 'What aspects of the situation do I have any control over?' Or ask yourself if there's any way you can think differently about the situation – is there a positive aspect to the situation?
- You can choose to focus on either what went wrong or what you can now do that's right. What's your choice?

The ability to accept small things not only makes everyday life less stressful, but by accepting the small things, you will then be better placed to manage the more difficult situations, such as your child's temper tantrums, your teenager's challenging behaviour, illness – yours or that of a family member – a missed opportunity, a sudden change in plans, not getting offered the job, the place on the course etc.

# Affirmations

Choose one of these affirmations to say to yourself when you need help accepting a situation:

- It is what it is.
- This is how it is.
- I accept things as they are instead of how I want them to be.
- I can't change what has already happened. I *can* change what happens from this moment on.
- It *is* possible for me to accept what happened and be ok.
- I accept what has happened. I can choose a new path.
- I don't understand why this happened, but I can accept that it did.

# Key points

- Acceptance is a way of thinking about and understanding something, yourself, someone else, an event or situation. Acceptance is the understanding that things have or haven't happened, or that things are or are not happening right now, and that things may or may not happen in the future.

- Acceptance brings a state of calm where you can rest without necessarily needing things to be different. What happens next, what you choose to do; that has to come out of your understanding of where you or the situation is right now. When you begin to accept the way things are now, rather than put up with a situation, resist it or fight it, you free your mind to move forward in positive ways.

- **Set yourself an intention:** If there's something that regularly irritates or annoys you, create an intention to use that irritation or annoyance as an opportunity to practise acceptance. Choose an accepting affirmation, such as 'It is what it is'. Repeat it to yourself. Whatever affirmation you choose, write it down now and leave it in places you will see it; maybe make it a screensaver message.

# Day 5

## AIM
To be more accepting of yourself.

## THOUGHT FOR TODAY
*When we accept who we are now, then we can change who we become.*

Mindful meditations encourage you to be aware of, acknowledge and accept your thoughts; to see them as separate entities and to let those thoughts pass.

Often, your thoughts will be about yourself. Those thoughts can be positive, encouraging and empowering. Your thoughts about an upcoming challenge, for example, could be 'I'll give it a try'. If you succeed, you might think 'I'm pleased with how I did that. Well done me!'

But your thoughts can also criticize and judge you, belittle and berate you. How often, for example, do you give yourself a hard time when you make a mistake or you screw up in some way? If you think you've upset someone or let someone down, perhaps you still feel guilty for whatever it was that you said or did. Do you blame yourself if things don't turn out the way you hoped? Or maybe you berate yourself when you're unable to cope with a particular situation. Perhaps you sometimes compare yourself with others and that leads you to having doubts about yourself, your abilities and your achievements.

---

## Exercise: Thoughts about yourself

Which of these thoughts have you had about yourself? In your journal, write down which of these thoughts you have ever had about yourself. Also, write down any other negative, critical thoughts you recall having had about yourself.

- I've made a mistake; I'm hopeless.
- I'm not a good friend/parent/brother/sister/daughter/son.
- I always say the wrong thing.
- People must think I'm stupid.
- Why can't I just be nice?
- I've screwed up. Again.
- I should have done better.
- I'm not going to be able to do this.
- What's the matter with me? Other people can do this. Why can't I?
- I'm not clever enough.

- I'm too fat/too thin/too short/too tall.
- I hate my nose/hair/feet (or some other part of your body).

Disapproving, critical thoughts about yourself erode your peace of mind and leave you feeling inadequate and hopeless. They don't allow room for self-acceptance.

---

### Exercise: I'm a lemon

Put this thought into your mind:

'I'm a lemon.'

Now put this thought into your mind:

'I'm hopeless.'

Which thought is easier to believe? You don't believe that you're a lemon, do you? Just because that thought was in your mind, doesn't mean you believe it. Unfortunately, it's easier to believe the thought that you are hopeless. But you don't have to believe that thought either.

---

## Being aware of thoughts about yourself

Your thoughts are so powerful because you rarely have conscious awareness of them. More often than not, you won't even notice when you're thinking in negative ways, berating and reprimanding yourself and bringing yourself down. However, practising 'open monitoring' meditation can help you be more aware of critical, disapproving thoughts about yourself.

And, in everyday situations, your emotions can also alert you to negative thoughts you may have about yourself. Whenever you're feeling worried or upset, stressed or angry about something you have or haven't done, or you feel disappointed with yourself, guilty or regretful about something you have or haven't done, stop and be aware of your thoughts.

41

## Exercise: Past situation

Think of a recent difficult, stressful event or situation for which you blamed or berated yourself. Maybe you lost or broke something. Perhaps you didn't manage to achieve something or you let someone down. Or you might have behaved badly towards someone else.

- In your journal, write down the situation. What were your thoughts likely to have been? Write them down.
- Read back over what your thoughts were. Did your thoughts make the situation easier in anyway? Did your thoughts help you feel better about yourself or the situation?
- Can you now see that you added to the pain of the situation with negative, berating thoughts about yourself?
- What do you think would have been a more helpful thought? In your journal, write down more positive, helpful thoughts.

# Recognizing that critical thoughts aren't helping you

Whenever you catch yourself thinking negative thoughts about yourself, as you have learned by doing the 'open monitoring' meditation try to step back from your thoughts and see them as separate entities.

Instead of saying, for example, 'I'm going to fail' say, '*I'm having the thought that* I'm going to fail', thereby creating some space between yourself and the thought.

Be aware of how you feel as a result of your thoughts – is it better or worse? Are your thoughts making an already difficult situation worse? Are your thoughts just adding to the pain and creating more suffering?

Ask yourself, 'In what way are these thoughts helping me?'

If, for example, after a period of time you're still reproaching yourself for having failed an exam, or an interview, see if you can take a step back and say to yourself, 'I'm having a thought that I'm hopeless. I'm never going to do well.' Then ask yourself, in what way is thinking like this helpful?

You can then choose whether to dwell on your negative thoughts and make your suffering worse or move on to more positive, encouraging and helpful thoughts – thoughts about what you can do now, in the present, to make a situation better.

## Self-kindness and compassion

Even if you have screwed up, made a mistake or made a fool of yourself in some way, there's always a different, kinder, better way to treat yourself that doesn't involve negative labels and self-criticism.

This is what Shauna Shapiro, who you read about in Day 4, discovered at the retreat in Thailand.

Having concluded that she was 'a terrible meditator,' and that 'meditation must be for other, more spiritual, calmer kinds of people', she was about to give up, when a monk explained to her the true meaning of mindfulness: heartfulness. He explained that true mindfulness involves an attitude of kindness and compassion. Instead of becoming frustrated and berating herself when her mind wandered, Shauna could actually hold the experience in compassionate awareness – just as she would be encouraging and kind to anyone else who was finding it difficult to meditate.

Shauna says that 'Understanding this connection between mindfulness and compassion has been transformational, helping me embrace myself and my experience with greater kindness and care.'

## Acceptance and commitment

In the practice of mindfulness, there is a concept known as 'acceptance and commitment' that can help you let go of unhelpful thoughts and move on to helpful thoughts. An acceptance and commitment approach suggests that you notice and *accept* a situation. You then move on – *commit* yourself – to more helpful ways of thinking, responding and behaving.

Supposing, for example, you were thinking, 'I've made a right mess of this. I'm hopeless.' You don't look for evidence that you've *not* made a mess of things and that you're *not* hopeless. Whether your thinking is correct or not – you simply acknowledge and *accept* that it's not helping you to continue thinking in this way and you move on to thinking – to *committing* yourself to more helpful thoughts and solutions.

So, in this example, you'd accept that maybe you did or maybe you didn't make a mess of something, and maybe you are or maybe you aren't hopeless. Whatever. The important thing would be to *accept* that what's done is in the past and think about how you could move on from there – what you could *commit* to doing now, in the present, to move forward in a positive way.

Acceptance and commitment recognizes that when you accept and let go of negative unhelpful thoughts, you let go of the emotional aspects and allow the rational, logical part of your mind to start working for you, to think in more helpful, positive ways.

Be mindful; know that all the time you are berating yourself for something that happened yesterday, days, weeks, months or even years ago, you are living in the past; you're letting the hurt and pain burden you by holding onto it. And that's not being kind or compassionate to yourself.

## Exercise: Self-compassion

Go back to the recent difficult, stressful event you identified and wrote about in the previous exercise. Whatever you did or didn't do, and however hard on yourself you were, think about what you would say to someone else in the same situation to make them feel better.

- What kind, helpful things would you say to a friend?
- How would you reassure them?
- What would you suggest they do to accept what did or didn't happen?
- What would you suggest they commit themselves to doing from now on?

Now, do that for yourself. Write it in your journal – what would you say to yourself?

# The power of 'but'

*'The longer we dwell on our misfortunes, the greater is their power to harm us.'*

Voltaire

A useful way to move on from negative, unhelpful thoughts to more helpful thoughts is to follow the negative thought with a 'but' and then complete the sentence. So, whenever you catch yourself saying something negative about yourself, add the word 'but'. This prompts you to follow up with a positive sentence.

'I've let my friend down because I forgot about meeting up with him this evening, *but* I could rearrange a date and offer to pick him up and buy the drinks.'

'I didn't do well in the interview, *but* I've learned something useful for the next interview.'

## Self-acceptance in the present moment

Self-acceptance happens in the present. It's not future oriented, as in 'I'll feel good about myself when ...' or 'As soon as I achieve or succeed with ... I'll be ok'. With self-acceptance you can absolutely accept where you are at any given moment, while also holding space for being more, for example, patient, careful or understanding. For being a better parent, friend or whatever it is you would like to be.

Accepting where you're at and that you're ok doesn't mean you can't move forward. It means that you recognize there are times when, just like everyone else, you won't be, for example, tactful or polite or show appreciation, that there are times when you'll say something hurtful, or be rude or thoughtless.

## Affirmations

Affirmations are positive statements; short brief sentences that you can assert to be true. Do they work?

45

Yes!

Thoughts such as 'I'm hopeless' or 'I look like shit' or 'I've screwed up again' are negative affirmations – negative thoughts that we have about ourselves. Often, we continue to repeat these negative affirmations to ourselves and, in so doing, establish beliefs about ourselves that – consciously or not – we believe to be true.

Positive affirmations about ourselves work in the same way. If we repeat them often enough, we will believe them to be true.

The affirmations that are going to be most effective and beneficial are the affirmations that resonate with you the most; that reflect what you want to be true. It's important that, when you choose an affirmation, you can believe it. It has to be realistic and plausible. An affirmation such as 'I'm the most beautiful, most clever person in the world' is probably not something you are going to believe to be true. Are you?

Choose one or more of the affirmations below or make up your own. Find what statements speak to you. Simple affirmations work best because they're easy to remember and get right to the point. Use language that feels right for you. Then, with each affirmation you have chosen, today, in your journal, write it out three times.

You could also write one or more of these affirmations on a sticky note that you put somewhere you can easily see it. Each time you read the words, pause for a few seconds and consider what the affirmation is telling you.

- I don't have to be so hard on myself.
- I made a mistake. Berating myself just makes things worse.
- It's okay to make mistake. I can let it pass and move on.
- My past does not determine my future.
- I accept my mistakes, but they don't define me.
- Like everyone else, I have both strengths and weaknesses.
- I am a person of worth, doing the best I can with what I know and what I have.
- I am a work in progress.
- I *will* treat myself with kindness.
- Every day is a new beginning. Take a deep breath and start again.

# Key points

- Self-acceptance involves recognizing that mistakes you have made and limitations you may have do not define you. Negative, self-berating thoughts are unhelpful and only serve to add more pain.

- An acceptance and commitment approach encourages you to be aware of thinking negative thoughts about yourself. You can step back and see those thoughts as separate from you. You don't have to believe them. You then let those thoughts go and commit to thinking more positive, helpful thoughts.

- **Set yourself an intention**: Choose one or two affirmations to memorize. Then, whenever you realize you are berating yourself, replace the negative thoughts with your chosen affirmations and more positive, helpful thoughts.

# Day 6

## AIM
To be aware of and accept feelings and emotions.

## THOUGHT FOR TODAY
*'But feelings can't be ignored, no matter how unjust or ungrateful they seem.'*

*Anne Frank*

Just as mindful meditations can help you to become more aware and accepting of your thoughts, mindful meditations can also help you be more aware and accepting of your emotions.

Whether we're aware of them or not, emotions are a constant presence in our lives. Emotions cause us to feel, think and act in different ways in different situations. And sometimes, our emotions can overwhelm us and lead us to react in ways that are unhelpful and can make a situation worse.

## Being aware of emotional triggers

We all have emotional triggers – specific situations and experiences that provoke a strong emotional reaction. Pleasant experiences and exciting situations and events can trigger emotions that make us feel good, but difficult situations and experiences can trigger difficult emotions that leave us feeling bad.

Often, when something happens to trigger an emotion, such as humiliation, guilt or jealousy, we react in unhelpful ways. Maybe, for example, when you feel humiliated you react by shouting and accusing, or you are silent and seething. Perhaps, if you feel guilty about something, you continually berate yourself about it, or you feel that you have to justify to yourself and others what you did or didn't do. And maybe, if you are jealous of someone, you react in mean and nasty ways, or you strongly deny to yourself and anyone else that you are jealous.

Particular situations can trigger a strong emotional reaction. It's different for each of us. Maybe your child refusing to eat their dinner or disapproval from your parents are likely to provoke a strong emotion. For someone else, it could be being asked to work overtime again, or something not working on the computer, or being kept on hold on the phone by a service provider.

## Exercise: Identify your emotional triggers

If you're unaware of your emotional triggers, your reactions can seem automatic and out of your control. Learning to recognize your own personal emotional triggers is the first step to being aware of and able to manage your unconscious, automatic reactions.

You can't predict every situation, but there are some that you know will push your buttons. Write down any trigger situations in your journal. For example:

- What makes you feel stressed?
- What can suddenly make you angry?
- What immediately frustrates you?
- What sort of situations leave you feeling resentful?
- What fills you with anxiety?
- What situations and circumstances leave you feeling disappointed?
- What situations leave you feeling embarrassed or humiliated?

Over the next few days, add any other situations that occur to you, that trigger a strong emotional reaction.

Next, identify and write down any of the following situations that trigger a strong emotional reaction. How do you react when you:

- are unfairly blamed
- are judged
- are criticized
- feel unwelcome
- have been lied to
- are ignored or rejected
- sense unfairness
- know that others are being treated badly
- are unsure and uncertain?

Now think about the situations that make you more vulnerable to being emotionally triggered. These might be when:

- you're tired
- you're hungry
- you've had too much to drink
- you're stressed.

These are times and situations where, when you encounter a trigger, you won't have as much control over your emotions. Until you pay attention, you may never have really noticed that whenever you are hungry, for example, you are more easily triggered.

# Being aware of an emotion in the moment

*'Emotions say hurry. Wisdom says wait.'*

*Author unknown*

Notice how, by doing the exercises today, you've been able to calmly identify the situations that trigger an emotional reaction in you. There is a space between you and the situations. And a space between you and the emotion. Unfortunately though, in the heat of the moment you probably won't identify an emotional trigger until after it's pulled!

Once you're more aware of the sort of situations that you know will trigger strong emotions, mindfulness can help you dial down and manage those emotions.

First though, it's helpful to know that there are three aspects to emotions: thoughts, physical feelings and behaviour. Each and any of these aspects can alert you to your emotions.

- **Thoughts:** such as 'How dare he!', 'Oh no! I feel awful' or 'For God's sake!'
- **Physical feelings:** feeling tense, rapid, shallow breathing, rapid heartbeat.
- **Behaviour:** crying, or raising your voice and snapping at other people.

As soon as you notice that you are reacting emotionally – you are aware of a change in your thoughts, physical feelings or behaviour – you need to do something to dial it down. Emergencies aside, most situations need clear, calm thinking rather than blind, emotional reactions. Rather than react automatically, you need to be able to stop and think calmly so that you can respond in a mindful, purposeful way; a way that doesn't make things worse.

Managing the physical feelings is a good start. This is where mindful breathing can help.

## Exercise: Focused counting meditation

Think of a recent occasion when you felt upset or angry about something; something that, at the time, triggered a reaction. Spend a minute remembering what happened. Now focus on your breathing for just one or two minutes.

- Stop breathing for three seconds (to 'reset' your breath).
- Next, breathe in slowly for three seconds and then breathe out more slowly – for five seconds. Be aware that it's the out breath that will slow everything down.
- Continue focusing on breathing in to a slow count of three and out to a slow count of five. Do this for a minute or two.

Just as with an 'open monitoring' meditation, with a focused counting meditation, you're aiming to create a space where you bring your attention to your breathing. Having to count as you breathe in to three, and then out to five, can really help keep your mind focused on your breathing.

Spending even a short amount of time – a minute or so just focusing on your breathing – breathing just a little slower and more deeply than normal helps to slow down the heartrate and thus shift your brain away from the fight, flight or freeze response that hijacks your ability to think clearly. It won't completely dispel the emotion – the anxiety, anger, guilt or jealousy – but it will slow everything down and bring you to a calmer place. When you are calm, you are able to think more clearly and respond to the situation more calmly.

## THE SCIENCE

Whether it's a medical test or an interview, an argument with someone, missing the bus or train or a delayed flight that triggers an emotional reaction, mindful breathing can help you be less physically and emotionally reactive to stressful events.

It helps to understand why and how this happens.

The body's automatic stress response is controlled by the autonomic nervous system. There are two aspects to our autonomic nervous system – the sympathetic nervous system and the parasympathetic nervous system. The sympathetic nervous system prepares your body to react quickly to threats and stress and go into fight, flight or freeze mode. Stress hormones such as cortisol are released. This results in increased blood pressure, heartrate and breathing.

When the danger or challenging situation has passed, the parasympathetic nervous system kicks in to slow things down; to lower your heartrate, blood pressure, breathing and stop the release of hormones such as cortisol, allowing you to recover from the stressful event – the anger, frustration, anxiety etc. – and for your mind and body to return to normal.

With mindfulness, you actually have the power to consciously access the parasympathetic nervous system. When you feel stressed – irritated, impatient, upset, angry or anxious – your sympathetic nervous system is in control. When you practise mindfulness meditation, you activate your parasympathetic nervous system, which dials everything down.

Faster breathing is the body's way of getting ready to either flee or fight. Practising mindful breathing helps you calm down because the slow, even breathing mimics the feeling of already being calm and able to think clearly and rationally. The breathing sends the message to your brain that all is ok. Your brain is then able to send the same message to your body, which will help to reduce your heartrate, lower your blood pressure and maintain the steady, even breathing.

You're not trying to change the emotion or stop yourself from feeling it, you're simply lessening the intensity.

Once you've calmed down, you're in a position to acknowledge and accept whatever you are feeling.

# Open monitoring meditation

With an 'open monitoring' meditation, you focus on your breathing. Then when you are aware that a thought has come into your mind, you step back and acknowledge it.

This approach can also help you to manage heightened emotions.

Focus on your breathing for just one to two minutes. When an emotional thought comes into your head, say to yourself 'I'm experiencing anger' or 'Here's a feeling of anxiety' or 'I'm feeling stressed.' There's no need to suppress the emotion, you just experience the feeling but without being overwhelmed or stuck in it.

Next time a situation occurs that provokes an emotion, try to identify the emotion you are having. Can you give the emotion a name – frustration? jealousy? shame? Instead of thinking, for example, 'It's not fair', a mindful observation might be 'Hmm, I am feeling frustration and resentment' or 'I'm feeling humiliated and embarrassed'.

See the emotion for what it is without judging it or attempting to get rid of it.

Rather than judging your emotions as good or bad, simply feel them and observe them. This is different from denying the emotion or trying to control the feeling; it's simply stepping back for a moment and seeing your emotion from a distance; seeing the emotion as a separate entity.

---

### Exercise: 'Open monitoring' meditation to manage emotions

Recall an occasion when you felt upset or angry about something. Spend a minute remembering what happened. What emotion or emotions did you experience?

Now focus on your breathing for just one to two minutes.

Whatever the feelings, acknowledge them. Say to yourself 'I'm experiencing anger' or 'Here's a feeling of anxiety' or 'I'm feeling stressed'. There's no need to suppress the emotion, you just experience the feeling but without being overwhelmed or stuck in it.

Try to view the feelings with a kind, compassionate awareness.

## Accepting your emotions

Accepting your emotions means simply understanding that right now, you feel like you do, whatever the reason.

Suppose, for example, you've just been let down – a friend cancels meeting you at the last moment (again). You feel resentful; you're frustrated and feel taken for granted. You are annoyed that your friend 'made' you feel like this.

Instead of blaming your friend for how you feel, a mindful approach encourages you to acknowledge and accept your feelings by saying to yourself, 'I'm feeling disappointed and frustrated. And that's ok. It's ok for me to feel this way.' Just being aware of and observing an emotion can help prevent you from being overwhelmed by it. You avoid being pulled back and forth, you are anchoring yourself to the present moment.

You simply let the emotion be there, without trying to change the feeling, the experience or the event that prompted it. You are already upset. Why exacerbate the stress? Whatever you're feeling, acceptance relieves you of needless extra suffering.

## Feeding the tiger

Once there lived an old man who kept many different kinds of animals. Two tigers that lived together in one cage particularly intrigued the old man's grandson. The tigers had different temperaments; one was calm and gentle and accepting whilst the other was unpredictable, mean and aggressive.

'Do they ever fight, Grandfather?' asked the boy.
'Occasionally, yes they do,' admitted the old man.
'And which one wins?'
*'Well, that depends on which one I feed the most.'*

Being able to manage an emotion depends, in part, on how much you 'feed' the emotions. No matter the situation, there's always more than one way to think and respond. Keep in mind that feeding an emotion is like feeding the difficult tiger – it can cause further distress and makes things worse.

It's a strategic *acceptance*; you may not like what's happening and how you are feeling, but by *accepting* a situation and the emotions it provoked, you free your mind to think more clearly.

The less you resist what is happening within you emotionally, the more opportunity you have to be present for the emotion and the positive message it is sending you. You observe and then respond to the message the emotion is sending you in a more mindful way. On Day 14 you will learn more about the positive messages that *all* emotions convey.

## Affirmations

Read through the list of affirmations. Choose one or two that resonate with you, that you can tell yourself when you feel emotionally charged:

- Be here, now.
- And breathe.
- I can breathe my way through this.
- It's ok to feel this way.
- It's ok to have strong feelings. I don't have to react immediately.
- I'm not okay right now, and that's okay.
- These feelings *will* pass.
- I am going to focus on my breathing until I know how best to respond.

# Key points

- Emotions cause us to feel, think and act in different ways in different situations. Difficult situations and experiences can trigger difficult emotions that leave you feeling bad; your emotions can overwhelm you and lead you to react in ways that are unhelpful and can make a situation worse.

- A mindful breathing meditation can help calm you down, re-engage your brain and allow you to collect and clarify your thoughts. You can then acknowledge and accept how you are feeling. And then you can move on to responding calmly and rationally.

- **Set yourself an intention:** Be aware of the sort of situations and experiences that, for you, trigger difficult emotions. Know that practising 'open monitoring' meditation trains your mind to acknowledge and accept difficult thoughts and emotions.

# Day 7

## AIM
To be accepting of other people; their thoughts, beliefs, opinions and behaviour.

## THOUGHT FOR TODAY
*'God grant me the serenity to accept the things I cannot change, courage to change the things I can, and the wisdom to know the difference.'*

*Serenity Prayer*

In the 'Serenity Prayer' (today's thought for today) we ask for the serenity to accept the things that we cannot change. And with other people that's often quite a lot!

What makes it easier to be accepting of other people is an attitude of non-judgement. Being non-judgemental means that rather than see something, yourself, another person, a situation, as 'good' or 'bad', 'right' or 'wrong', you just experience or observe it as it is.

Do you make judgements about other people? Of course you do. We all do. We're human! We judge, assess, form opinions and come to conclusions about others – about their words, their opinions, beliefs and actions.

We judge things that other people do that we don't approve of – the person your friend has chosen to marry for example, or the way your brother brings up his children. A colleague taking too long with a lunch break, or the way your partner loads the dishwasher.

We often struggle to accept other people's choices, opinions and beliefs, actions and behaviour as valid and worthy. We judge and make assumptions about what other people do that we don't understand or approve of.

But when we're judging someone else, we're not accepting them.

---

### Exercise

How can you be more accepting of others? First you need to be aware that you're being judgemental.

Think about whether, in the last week, someone else's words, opinions or actions have:

- irritated or annoyed you
- disappointed you
- left you feeling impatient or frustrated with them
- filled you with resentment.

Think about the people you know – friends, family, colleagues – as well as the people you don't know – drivers, call centre workers, people in shops and on public transport, celebrities and politicians.

Write in your journal what it was about each person and what they said or did that you didn't like that disappointed, frustrated or annoyed you.

---

# Accepting not extending dislike and disapproval

It's normal to disagree with someone or want them to behave differently, but too often this can tip over into fault-finding, righteousness, resistance, anger or berating. When you do this, you're just adding to your pain. You already don't like what they've said or done. That's ok. You don't have to like it. But it doesn't help you (or them) when you prolong or exacerbate and embitter the disagreement, dislike or disapproval by railing against what they've said or done, or by thinking how stupid, unfair, mean or nasty they are being.

Instead, you accept that you may not like what they've done or said, you may feel upset or angry about it, but you can recognize that *is* what they are like or it *is* what they think or it *is* what they've done. You understand that you cannot make them change. And then you move on to thinking how best to respond.

You might choose not to respond at all; you might just walk away. Or, it might be appropriate to negotiate with the other person, challenge them or do something to protect yourself or others. Either way, know that all the time you are unable to accept them, you have given them all the power; the ability to upset or anger you. Once you accept a person and the way they are, you take responsibility for how you feel.

## Accepting differences between you and someone else

Nikita spent last weekend staying with her friend Jan. Nikita is an early riser but Jan is not. Nikita had a choice: she could become irritated with Jan for sleeping in until late morning rather than spending the morning with her, or she could accept their different sleeping patterns and do something on her own for the first few hours of the day.

On this occasion, Nikita noticed her irritation, and allowed it to be there without feeding it. Instead, she lay listening to music, read the book she had brought with her and took a short walk. When Jan got up, the day continued and they had a lovely afternoon together.

Suffering arises in the gap between what we want and what we get. By letting go of the expectation that she would get to share a morning with Jan, Nikita was able to accept the experience just as it was and go with it, allowing the weekend to unfold.

Like Nikita, you probably have friends who behave in ways you find difficult – maybe they are chronically late for everything. You can get irritated by this or you can simply accept that this is the way this person is and find a way to accommodate it.

## Accepting the unacceptable

Is it possible – realistic even – to accept anyone and everyone?

What if they reveal racist views? Or sexist, misogynistic or homophobic views? What if they have political opinions or religious beliefs that are totally at odds with yours? What if they've committed crimes? What if they've harmed someone else? How can you accept them then?

Accepting people does not mean agreeing with them, approving of them, waiving your own rights, or downplaying their impact upon you or someone else.

Accepting their views or actions means that you recognize that they are thinking or behaving, or have done, in a particular way. You know that railing against them or berating them isn't going to change them. You don't have to accept what they've said or done but you can accept that, for whatever reason, they have done or still do behave in certain ways. Acceptance is not approval. It could be that events and experiences in their life have brought them to who they are now. You might choose to consider this. You might choose not to respond at all; you might just walk away. Or, it may be appropriate to challenge them or do something to protect yourself or others.

## Exercise: Raise your awareness

By being more aware of what you find difficult to accept about other people, you can practise being more accepting. Which of the following behaviours and attitudes in other people irritates, frustrates, upsets or annoys you? In your journal, write down any of the following behaviours and attitudes you find difficult to accept. Add any others you think of.

- lateness
- untidiness
- not doing their fair share of work
- stubbornness
- laziness
- impatience
- being slow to act
- bad habits – drinking, smoking or taking drugs

Where there's a will, there's a way. You *can* accept that others behave or think in ways you don't approve of or agree with. Remind yourself that railing against them saying 'I can't believe they are like this. What's the matter with them? Why are they like this? What are they trying to do?' just extends your pain. Instead, step back from these thoughts and move on to thinking of an appropriate response.

## Popular misconception

The words 'acceptance' and 'tolerance' are not synonymous; they don't mean the same thing. Acceptance is not the same as tolerance. When it comes to accepting or tolerating another person, if you tolerate them, you reluctantly put up with someone or an aspect of a person. Tolerance involves enduring someone else. Acceptance is kinder than tolerance. Acceptance is a state of goodwill – a patient, benign attitude and approach. Acceptance involves recognizing that right now, someone is, has or will be. And that's ok.

## Try it now

Practise responding with *acceptance*. Next time you read in a newspaper or magazine, or listen – on the radio, TV or overhear in public – to someone else's opinion and it annoys you, accept it. Recognize that they simply think differently from you.

# Be curious, not judgemental

'Be curious. Not judgemental.'

*Walt Whitman*

Very often, you don't even need to understand why someone thinks or behaves in the way they do. You just need to accept. It *is* possible to accept without understanding. You can choose not to challenge them, say anything or respond in any way. And that's ok.

Or you could find out more. Instead of being judgemental, be curious. Make the effort to learn and know more about someone, whatever aspect of them you're struggling to accept – a view, belief or opinion they have, an action or behaviour.

Often, our judgements about others are because they do or say things we find difficult to understand. We see something someone does or listen to what someone says that we don't approve of or agree with and we become critical and judgemental. We have ideas of what they 'should' be doing or thinking and the way they are 'supposed' to do things. We judge their choices as 'wrong'. And that's the end of it. We don't try to find out more. We don't try to understand. It doesn't occur to us that they are simply thinking or behaving in a different way than we would.

Here's an invitation. Replace judgement with curiosity. Mindfulness encourages us to be curious; to replace judgement with curiosity. Ask yourself what could be a reasonable explanation for why they've done or said what they did? Believe something good about someone, rather than something bad.

Replacing judgement with curiosity is more likely to lead to acceptance. So, from now on, when someone else's words, opinions or actions leave you feeling irritated, impatient, disappointed or even angry with them, avoid judging them. Be curious instead.

## Five differences between judgement and curiosity

1. Judgement feels closed. Curiosity feels open.
2. Judgement sees things as facts: 'He doesn't know what he's talking about.' 'She's a waste of time.' 'They obviously don't care.' Curiosity see things in terms of unknowns: 'I wonder why?' 'What for?'
3. Judgement insists on 'should' and 'shouldn't', 'must' and 'mustn't'. Curiosity asks 'how come?' and 'why?'
4. Judgement is synonymous with the words intolerance, prejudice, discrimination and exclusion. Curiosity is synonymous with the words interested, listening, concerned, communication and connection.
5. Curiosity doesn't know, and is interested to find out more. Judgement has already decided.

Whether it's what someone likes to eat and drink, the clothes they wear or where they go on holiday, or other people's different customs, beliefs or religions, everyone, in some way is different from you. You don't have to like their differences but you can accept them.

## A parent's story

When Ali's son JoJo was a teenager, she spent a lot of time and effort trying to get him to be more tidy, to do better at maths and to enjoy reading. Ali believed she just wanted the best for her son; that her efforts to get him to do 'better' was as a result of her love for him.

One day, after an argument with her son about reading, it occurred to Ali that the things she wanted for JoJo gave him the message that she didn't accept him.

'Was I making him feel like he was not OK just how he was?' she asked herself.

Yes, he wasn't very tidy or organized, maths wasn't his strong point and he didn't share the same love for reading that she had. Ali realized that accepting this didn't mean she didn't love JoJo or that she'd 'given up' on him. Instead, it meant that she could recognize that being untidy, maths not being his strong point and not enjoying reading was just who he was.

Focusing on issues around JoJo's untidiness, maths and reading eroded Ali's relationship with him and prevented her from focusing on his strengths.

When we accept others as they are, we are also encouraging them to accept themselves.

## Try it now

Allow others to be different. Notice how often you use the phrases 'that's wrong' or 'you're wrong'. What if they are just different? What would happen if you stopped seeing others in terms of right and wrong? Would life be easier or more difficult?

## Affirmations

- I can accept the way others think or behave. I don't have to approve or agree.
- Acceptance is a state of goodwill and grace.
- Right now, someone (name the person) is, has or will be. And that's ok.
- Be curious. Not judgemental.

# Key points

- What makes it easier to be accepting of other people is an attitude of non-judgement. Being non-judgemental means that rather than see something, yourself, another person, a situation, as 'good' or 'bad', 'right' or 'wrong', you just experience or observe it as it is.

- Accepting people does not mean agreeing with them, approving of them, waiving your own rights, or downplaying their impact upon you or someone else. Accepting their views or actions means that you recognize that they are thinking or behaving, or have done, in a particular way. You know that railing against them or berating them isn't going to change them. You might choose to find out more, or not to respond at all; you might just walk away. Or, it may be appropriate to challenge them or be necessary to do something to protect yourself or others.

- **Set yourself an intention:** Mindfulness encourages us to be curious – to replace judgement with curiosity. What could be a reasonable explanation for why someone has done or said what they did? Believe something good about someone, rather than something bad.

# Day 8

## AIM
To develop mindful compassion for others.

## THOUGHT FOR TODAY
*'Be kind, for everyone you meet is fighting a harder battle.'*

*Plato*

As well as judging other people's opinions and beliefs, behaviour and actions as unacceptable, if we think that their beliefs, choices or behaviour have resulted in them suffering a misfortune, we don't always find it easy to be sympathetic. If we believe that a person's predicament is their own fault, we are likely to respond with criticism and judgement.

Perhaps, in the past, you've been dismissive about a person's plight, and thought that the difficulties they were suffering they brought on themselves. Or maybe you currently know someone who is struggling in some way, but they won't take advice and they don't seem to be doing anything to help themselves. You don't find it easy to think kindly about them. You think they should get a grip and change their ways.

Whenever you've responded to someone else's circumstances with feelings such as irritation, impatience or disappointment, then you've probably judged them too.

Usually, another person's suffering invites compassion – compassion being the sadness and sympathy we feel, accompanied by a strong desire to help. But being critical and judgemental leaves no room for kindness and compassion.

## Exercise: Other people's misfortune

Think of someone you know, or have heard or read about, who has done something that resulted in them suffering a loss, difficulty or hardship. Perhaps they:

- took part in a high-risk sport
- fell for a dating scam or a money scam
- chose not to take their medication or have a vaccination
- voted for an issue
- cheated on their partner
- gambled, drank excessively or took drugs
- didn't pay a parking fine
- committed a crime

- didn't leave enough time to be somewhere – the station or the airport, for example
- didn't revise for a test or an exam or do their homework.

When it became apparent that their choice resulted in them losing out or suffering in some way, how did you respond? In your journal describe what your thoughts were likely to have been about any of the situations that someone else experienced.

## Replace judgement with acceptance and compassion

We all have assumptions about others that prevent us from accepting their situations and their choices. We assume we know the whole story. But what if we can view other people's circumstances and choices with an open mind – a beginner's mind? (More about beginner's mind on Day 12.) What if you were able to show kindness and compassion to others without thinking about whether or not they deserve it? They do deserve it.

We are all different. You know that. Other people are simply managing a situation in a different way than you would. You don't have to agree with how they're doing it. But you can be accepting and show compassion if their choices lead to difficulties for them. Rather than assume and critically judge, have a kindly perspective, interpretation and understanding of someone else's difficulties and challenges. Even if they did bring it upon themselves.

## Meditation and compassion for others

On Day 5 you learned how meditation can help you practise self-compassion. Rather than become impatient and frustrated and berate yourself when you lose focus and your mind wanders, you were encouraged to be kind and patient with yourself. In this way, kindness and compassion become an intrinsic aspect of meditation.

As you continue to practise meditation, not only do you learn to have a kind, compassionate attitude towards yourself, the self-compassion you develop helps foster compassion towards others. In the practice of mindfulness, compassion reflects the idea that everything is related to everything else. Compassion allows us to see our interconnectedness; to be aware of the connection we have with everyone and everything.

How can you further develop compassion? By looking for what you share with people rather than what separates you from them.

## Exercise: Shared experiences

It often turns out you're judging someone for something that you yourself have done. Which of these situations have you experienced?

- You made a choice or decision that didn't turn out well.
- You didn't do something out of laziness and then missed out.
- You did something because you thought it would look or feel good but you later regretted it.
- You did something that left you ill or injured.
- You took on more than you could handle. You became overwhelmed and stressed.
- You were in a relationship or friendship that you knew to be no good – it turned out you were right.
- You spent a lot of time, money or effort on someone or something. It didn't end well.
- You failed at something others told you wasn't a good idea in the first place. You didn't listen.

If you have experienced one or more of these situations, in your journal, briefly describe what happened and your feelings at the time. Maybe you felt scared? Disappointed? Humiliated? Regretful?

# Popular misconception

You might think that in order to feel sympathy and compassion for someone, you need to have been in a similar situation facing the same difficulties, or at least be able to picture yourself in a similar situation, facing the same problems. This is not the case.

Certainly, if you *have* made the same choices and experienced, or can imagine experiencing, the same difficulties, you will probably find it easier to feel empathy and compassion. But empathy comes from identifying and relating to another person's *feelings* about a situation, not just from the situation itself.

## Exercise: Shared feelings and emotions

Each and everyone of us experiences difficult, distressing emotions. In your journal, note down situations where you have experienced each of these emotions.

- disappointment
- despair
- frustration
- stress
- regret
- guilt
- overwhelm
- fear and being scared
- loneliness
- worry and anxiety

# Recognizing and relating to the feelings of others

You don't have to have experienced exactly the same circumstances to be able to empathize with someone else. When you have empathy, the experience may be different but the resulting emotion is the same. You may not have made the same mistake as someone else but you probably have done something that left you feeling how *they* do right now – disappointed, for example, or regretful, guilty, or anxious. These are all emotions that, when experienced by someone, would usually prompt concern and sympathy, kindness and compassion from you.

With empathy, even if you can't relate to the experience, you can relate to the emotion. (A concept known as emotional resonance.) It then follows that having felt empathy, having recognized and understood the emotion that someone is feeling, you can more easily accept how they are feeling – that they are suffering – and show compassion.

It could be, for example, that you don't feel anxious about flying in an airplane. But you *have* experienced anxiety about a different situation. Your ability to empathize, then, with someone who is anxious about flying, comes from recognizing, understanding and relating to the emotion – to the anxiety.

Feeling empathy for someone who is suffering and connecting with their distress is an intrinsic part of understanding the universality of suffering in human experience. Compassion reflects the idea that, one way or another, everyone and everything is connected to everyone and everything else.

---

## Exercise: Show compassion

Mindfulness encourages you to be *aware* of your interactions with others – to be open to the difficulty, the struggle, the impact of events, the stress, sorrow and strain in others. And to respond with compassion.

- Who today, in your life could benefit from compassion? Someone who is lonely, unwell, worried and anxious about something? Someone you know who has recently suffered a loss of some kind?
- Be open to compassion for people you don't know: a harassed looking parent, a confused tourist, someone sleeping rough. Moments of compassion come in the flow of life. You can do something small each day to help – smile, give a kind word, make a supportive comment.

- Remember when someone has shown you compassion, when they extended a kind, caring concern to you when you were in distress or suffering in some way. What did they do that helped?
- What do you think a person who is struggling, who is distressed, might find helpful? Ask them. Ask if you can help. People often find it difficult to ask for help. They feel that they are inconveniencing the other person or being a burden. The next time you know of or see someone who looks down or frustrated, offer to help them. Simply ask how you could help make a situation better.
- If you have already thought of something you could do that might help, it might be appropriate to ask first, if they are ok with you helping out in that way.

## DID YOU KNOW?

In Buddhism, developing compassion – making an effort to alleviate the suffering experienced by others – is one of the ways to achieve enlightenment or nirvana.

The Buddhist figure most focused on kindness and compassion is the bodhisattva of compassion, known originally as Avalokiteshvara, who became popular in India in the sixth century AD. Avalokiteshvara is most often depicted as having 11 heads and 1,000 arms, which he uses to benefit all sentient beings. Tibetan Buddhists believe that all Dalai Lamas are manifestations of this bodhisattva.

Bodhisattvas are enlightened beings on the path towards Buddhahood, who have put off entering paradise in order to help others attain enlightenment. The bodhisattva of compassion is known by various names across Asia. In China, the bodhisattva is a female figure called Guanyin and portrayed as a woman with long, flowing hair, wearing a robe, who holds a vase tilted downwards so she can pour the drops of compassion upon all beings.

# Loving kindness meditation

Some of the earliest Buddhist teachings developed in India emphasized the idea of *metta* or loving kindness. The Buddha exhorts 'the good and wise' to spread loving kindness by making wishes of goodwill towards all beings.

A loving kindness meditation can help raise your awareness for compassion and empathy. It involves bringing to mind someone you love, and expressing the hope that they are safe, well, and happy.

You then extend the sentiment outward to those around you.

## Exercise: Loving kindness meditation

You can follow this simple loving kindness practice.

Bring to mind a person in your life who you care about; someone you like, are fond of or someone you love.

What good things do you wish for them? Your wish for them might be that they are happy, feel connected to others, are kind to themselves, that they are healthy in body and mind. The person you are thinking of may currently be struggling or experiencing difficulties and challenges in their life. So you might wish that they experience healing and wellness, that they be free from fear. That they experience peace and calm. You might wish that someone experiences being loved, supported and encouraged.

In your journal write down whoever you are thinking of and whatever you wish for them.

Now, imagine them sitting in front of you. Focus on your breathing for a minute or two and then, out loud or in your mind say to this person what it is that you have written down that you wish for them. You might, for example say about someone who is about to start a new phase in their life 'May you feel welcomed and included. May you feel understood and supported. May you be content and happy.'

You can extend this loving kindness to someone in your life who you have had difficulty with. Someone you're currently feeling frustrated, irritated or annoyed with.

It's not going to be easy, but try and think of something good that you wish for them. It could be that you wish that they have more understanding and patience. Or that they move on with their life. Again write down what you wish for them and then imagine them sitting in front of you. Focus on your breathing for a minute or two and then, with the same intention and goodwill that you had for the person who you care for, say to them what you wish for them.

Know now, that regularly practising loving kindness meditations trains your mind to be more understanding – thoughtful, kind, and compassionate towards other people.

## Affirmations

Choose one or more of these affirmations, to say to yourself whenever you are aware that someone else needs compassion:

- Everyone, myself included, is deserving of kindness and compassion.
- I look to be aware of and support the wellbeing of others.
- I strive to have empathy and understanding for others.
- I look for and relate to the emotion someone is feeling.
- I treat others as I would like them to treat me.
- There is often something I can do to make things better.
- I look to make a positive difference to others.

# Key points

- Compassion is the sadness and sympathy we feel, accompanied by a strong desire to help a person or animal who for whatever reason, has experienced misfortune and is suffering in some way.

- You can develop compassion by looking for what you share with other people rather than what separates you from them. You may or may not be able to relate to their situation, but you can relate to how they are feeling – upset, anxious or scared, for example. In other words, you can empathize. Empathy makes it easier to accept how they are feeling – that they are suffering – and show compassion.

- **Set yourself an intention:** Today, extend your compassion. Think of someone who could benefit from some kindness and empathy. Maybe you know someone who is lonely or unwell, worried and anxious about something. Is there someone you know who has recently suffered a loss of some kind? What do you think the person to whom you are showing compassion might find helpful? If you're not sure, offer a couple of ideas and then ask them if you can help.

# Day 9

## AIM
To understand forgiveness; to accept and let go of someone else's wrongdoing.

## THOUGHT FOR TODAY
*Forgiveness doesn't change the past. But it does change the future.*

With an 'open monitoring' meditation, as you focus on your breathing, if you notice that a thought has come into your mind, you acknowledge it as just a thought. You are encouraged to accept it and let it go. Then you return your attention back to your breathing.

Acceptance and letting go are key aspects of forgiveness. Most of us regularly forgive other people. We forgive the person who held up the queue at the supermarket. We forgive the friend who forgot that they were meeting us for dinner that evening. We forgive the family member who spilt a drink on our sofa. We accept that it happened and we let it go.

These sorts of things are relatively easy to forgive and forget. But what if you are faced with more serious issues?

What if you've been deceived or lied to, humiliated or let down? When someone does something that really upsets or angers you it's not always easy to forgive them. It can feel like you're giving in, absolving the other person, freeing them from blame and letting them get away with it.

---

## Exercise: Acts of transgression

Have you ever experienced any of these situations? Or have you had any similar experience that you've found difficult to forgive someone else for? Think of an occasion when someone:

- took something or someone from you
- damaged or destroyed something that belonged to you
- caused you a serious injury
- harassed, bullied or abused you
- accused you of something you hadn't done
- did something that cost you a lot of money
- broke a contract
- failed to deliver or didn't come through
- hurt or injured someone you love
- died.

In your journal, write a brief description of what happened. Who-ever it was and whatever the situation, if you have forgiven them, note down how and why you have forgiven them. If you have not forgiven them, note down why not; why you have been unable to forgive them.

## Forgiving is not easy

It's not always easy to accept what happened and forgive the other person or people involved. And the situation can be made worse if you can't understand or get a clear answer as to why the other person did what they did. Perhaps you've been hurt by someone who showed no remorse or is now absent? A partner who left for someone else, or a parent who died without ever acknowledging the harm they inflicted, or a friend who betrayed a trust and then walked away?

You may feel that you deserve to know why they behaved that way. You want some level of understanding – a degree of closure. But often, other people don't apologize or explain why they did something. Then, not only do you have to accept what they did but also what they didn't do.

However, all the time you are blaming the other person for your feelings of sadness, bitterness or anger and are waiting for an explana-tion or an apology, you are doing two things:

- You are extending your pain and suffering.
- You are giving away your power – you are relying on their actions or inaction to make you feel better, or you are allowing their actions or inaction to make you feel worse.

So how can you stop being so hurt? With an acceptance and commit-ment approach. This means acknowledging what happened, accepting it, letting it go and moving on. Forgiveness means letting go of the distress, resentment or anger that you feel as a result of someone else's actions. It involves letting go of any thoughts you might have about punishment, revenge or compensation.

The most important thing to know is that forgiveness is, first and foremost, for your benefit, not the person who hurt or offended you. You've already been hurt once, you don't need to let the offence and your pain continue to hurt you by holding onto it.

Each time you think about what happened, each time you tell the story from the past, you relive it in the present. Mindfulness can help you to recognize this. It encourages you to recognize that all the time you are unable to forgive, you are living in the past; you are holding on to something that happened days, weeks, months or even years ago.

You are not responsible for the other person's thoughts and actions. But you *are* responsible for yours. You are responsible for your happiness and peace of mind. Understanding this can help you to look at forgiveness in a new light.

## Decisional forgiveness and emotional forgiveness

There are two different kinds of forgiveness: decisional forgiveness and emotional forgiveness.

Decisional forgiveness happens when you decide that, even though you may still feel negatively towards the other person, from now on, you will interact differently with them.

You might decide that you forgive them but you don't want them in your life anymore. On the other hand, you might decide you *will* continue your relationship or friendship with them, but first you reflect on what you have learned from the situation. Then you decide what conditions you will put in place to protect yourself; to make yourself less vulnerable and lessen the chances of their actions hurting you again.

This is an acceptance and commitment approach. You accept that what happened – what they did – cannot be changed (and you may have to accept that the other person may not recognize their wrongdoing or apologize) and you commit to interacting differently with them from now on.

Take, for example, this situation: a friend accuses you of breaking something that she lent you and demands that you pay for the damage. She tells other people about it too. You are hurt and upset by the unfair accusation. It wasn't you who broke the item. Some time later, your friend realizes this. However, in the meantime, you decide to keep the friendship but never to borrow anything from her in future. You begin again, but on a different basis.

Whereas decisional forgiveness happens when you make a change in the way you interact with the other person, emotional forgiveness happens when you change the way you *feel* toward the other person.

It means allowing sadness, bitterness and resentment to give way to understanding and feeling, for example, sympathy, empathy, or compassion. Again, you take an acceptance and commitment approach. You accept what happened and what they did and didn't do. You let go of feelings of sadness, anger and wanting recrimination. You understand that the pain may not ever go away completely, but even though it won't be easy, you commit to an understanding, compassionate approach.

*'Perhaps everything terrible is in its deepest being something that needs our love.'*

*Rainer Maria Rilke*

In the same example, you might recognize that what was behind your friend's reaction was the fact that what she lent you had huge emotional value or that she couldn't afford to get it mended. She was very anxious and stressed about it. As you learned in Day 8, someone else's anxiety and stress are emotions that, in other circumstances, would invite concern and compassion from you

## A story of forgiveness

When NYPD officer Steven McDonald entered New York's Central Park on the afternoon of 12 July 1986, he had no reason to expect anything out of the ordinary. However, after a confrontation with three teenage boys who were in the park that day, Steven was shot by one of them. The incident left him permanently paralysed from the neck down.

Telling his story in the book *Why Forgive?* by Johann Christoph Arnold, Steven explains that six months after he was shot, his wife gave birth to a baby boy. 'We named him Conor. To me, Conor's birth was like a message from God that I should live, and live differently. And it was clear to me that I had to respond to that message. I prayed that I would be changed, that the person I was would be replaced by something new.

That prayer was answered with a desire to forgive the young man who shot me. I wanted to free myself of all the negative, destructive emotions that his act of violence had unleashed in me: anger, bitterness, hatred, and other feelings. I needed to free myself of those emotions so that I could love my wife and our child and those around us. I forgave because I believe the only thing worse than receiving a bullet in my spine would have been to nurture revenge in my heart.'

Steven's move to free himself of anger, bitterness and hatred so that he could love his wife and their child and those around them embodied the concept of radical acceptance.

# Reminder

Being able to accept a situation and not extending the difficulties and challenges into further suffering is often referred to as 'radical acceptance'. Radical acceptance recognizes that with a difficult or unwanted situation, resisting and railing against it just makes things worse. Radical acceptance is a conscious decision to see things differently.

## Exercise: Learning how to forgive

If you have reached a point where you want to put someone else's actions behind you and move on with your life, writing about what happened is a positive step to processing the situation.

Write an honest, heartfelt letter telling the other person how you feel and how their actions affected you. You're not going to send the letter, but you *are* going to express your thoughts and feelings directly to the other person. There are several steps to take:

- Describe what happened. What were the circumstances that led to the situation? What was it that the other person did or didn't do? Write it all down.
- Acknowledge your feelings about what happened and how you felt at the time. As you write, allow yourself to feel upset, disappointed, frustrated or angry. If you feel like crying, then cry. Crying is cathartic; it helps relieve emotional tension. It unifies your thoughts, feelings and physical body.
- As well as writing about how you felt, you may also want to explain *why* you felt the way you did then.
- Explain how you feel now. Do you still feel the same? Are your feelings just as strong? Or do you feel differently?
- Think about what you learned from the experience. What would you do differently to avoid becoming involved in a similar situation? Write about how and why you have decided that you will (or won't) interact with them in future. Will your relationship continue as before? Or will you interact with them in a different way from now on?
- Explain your intentions to extend (or not extend) emotional forgiveness. Do you recognize that they behaved the way they did as a result of an inability, weakness or limitation they have?
- If you intend to extend emotional forgiveness, write an expression of goodwill towards them. You might also find that a loving kindness meditation (see Day 8 for this) helps you with emotional forgiveness.
- Stay present; let go of old narratives and painful pasts. From now on change the story you replay to yourself and to other people. Change your story to one that tells of your decision to forgive; that you've accepted the past can't be changed but that you have learned from what happened; you've let go and moved on. You are beginning again.

## Exercise: 'Open monitoring' meditation for forgiveness

An 'open monitoring' meditation can help you let go of distress, bitterness and unforgiving thoughts.

- As always, focus your attention on breathing in and breathing out. When you notice that a thought has come into your mind, before you go back to focusing on your breathing, *acknowledge* the thought.
- Tell yourself, 'A thought has come into my mind.' Tell yourself, for example, 'I've just had a thought about how badly the other person behaved towards me.' Then return your attention back to your breathing.

In this way, you are practising letting go of unforgiving thoughts. Try to let such thoughts come and go without judging them. Recognize them as natural and normal. Try not to force anything, or pretend to feel anything. It's ok if you don't feel a rush of peace, calm and forgiveness.

## Forgiveness takes time

Be patient. Give yourself time to heal. Know that letting go, acceptance and forgiveness are all part of a process that takes time. Sometimes your ability to forgive will come soon and easily. At other times it will take longer. Know that wherever you are right now, is okay.

Forgiveness can't be forced, you have to be drawn to it. But don't get stuck in resenting what happened and railing against it. Know that rumination – going over and over your feelings of sadness and disappointment or frustration and anger – do not have to go on forever. Know that when you let go, you create space for something better.

# Breathe

If, at any time you find yourself reminded of what happened or are overwhelmed by painful memories, ground yourself by using mindful breathing to help you to manage the moment. Say to yourself, 'Each time I breathe out, I let go.'

# Affirmations

- I may not understand but I do forgive.
- I forgive so that I can have peace.
- Forgiveness is a gift to myself.
- Forgiveness gives me a fresh start.
- The past does not define me. I choose to let go.
- No matter how difficult I find it to let go and forgive, the present is always here to remind me that I don't have to stay stuck in yesterday.
- Today I can choose to keep holding on. Or I can decide today is the day I will start to let go.
- I let go of the past actions of others, so that I can move forward and be free in the present.

# Key points

*'Getting over a painful experience is much like crossing monkey bars. You have to let go at some point in order to move forward.'*

C.S. Lewis

- Forgiveness means letting go of the distress, resentment or anger that you feel as a result of someone else's actions. It involves letting go of any thoughts you might have about punishment, revenge or compensation.

- Forgiveness is first and foremost, for your benefit, not the person who hurt or offended you. You've already been hurt once, you don't need to let the offence and your pain continue to hurt you by holding onto it.

- **Set yourself an intention**: If you've reached a point where you want to put someone else's actions behind you and move on with your life, writing about what happened is a positive step to processing the situation. Practise an 'open monitoring' meditation too, to help you let go of unforgiving thoughts.

# Day 10

## AIM
To let go of attachments that keep you unhappy.

## THOUGHT FOR TODAY
*'Begin doing what you want to do now. We are not living in eternity. We have only this moment, sparkling like a star in our hand, and melting like a snowflake.'*

*Francis Bacon*

Whether it's ditching joyless exercise classes, leaving a boring party or giving up on a novel or TV series because you just can't get into it, too often, instead of letting go of something that we're not enjoying, we feel we 'should' keep going, that we 'ought' to stick with it.

Letting go of these everyday occurrences is hard enough, but when it comes to bigger issues, like leaving a job you don't like, or calling time on a friendship or an unhappy relationship, it can be really difficult to let go and move on to better things.

Perhaps you now realize, for example, that you committed yourself to something too quickly; you didn't think it through properly. Or maybe what you thought you wanted to do then doesn't now seem such a good idea after all; new information has come to light and you realize there's a different path you could take. Perhaps your circumstances have changed and you have new options. It could be that what you'd rather do is more in line with your abilities; is more realistic and achievable for you. Maybe you've simply had a change of heart; your feelings about a situation have changed. Whatever it is, you don't find it easy to detach yourself and let go. Even though you are unhappy, you continue to remain with something or someone.

## Exercise: Identify a situation that makes you unhappy

In your journal, describe a situation that you are currently dissatisfied or unhappy with and that you'd rather no longer be part of. It could be something minor such as a book you are reading, or a TV series you have tried, or an exercise class that is no longer the right one for you. Or it could be something on the list below:

- **A job:** You don't like the work, it's boring or it's too stressful. You don't like the people you work with. You can't cope with the commute.

- **A course of study:** It's too difficult. It's the wrong course. You're stressed and unhappy. If it's away from home, you may be homesick.
- **A cause or voluntary work or a hobby:** You liked it at first, but you're not enjoying it now.
- **A lifestyle:** It could be being self-employed, running your own business, home schooling, being vegan. It was a good idea at the time. Now it's a drag.
- **A DIY project at home:** It's not going well. It's taking too long to complete.
- **A relationship or friendship:** It's run its course, you no longer have anything in common. Or worse, it's draining you. You're unhappy.
- **Where you live:** The home, the village, the town or city. For one reason or another, it's just not right for you.

## Exercise: Identify why you can't let go

Whatever it is that you are doing, what do you tell yourself is the reason you can't detach yourself and let go? Below are some possible reasons: In your journal, write down which of these reasons might be why you are unable to let go. Add any other reason you have for holding on to a situation.

- I've put up with it all for so long I might as well continue.
- I don't want to admit that I made the wrong decision in the first place.
- I don't want to face the fact that I've continued with something that's been making me unhappy for so long.
- I'm thinking about all the time, effort, love or money I've already put into it. What will have been the point of all that if I cut loose now?

- I'm worried about letting people down if I pull out; they'll be disappointed or upset, offended or even angry if I tell them I no longer want to be involved in something that they rely on me for or that they think I 'should' be doing.
- I can't see an alternative course of action. It's difficult to walk away; I can't see what other path to take.
- Walking away could mean quite a big change in my life.

Of course, you don't want to give up too easily on your commitments, but strength of character lies not only in our ability to persist with difficult situations, but in our ability to know when to call it a day. Refusing to let go of something that's making you miserable means you are allowing the past to dictate the present. And that's not being mindful!

## Having regrets

Palliative care nurse Bronnie Ware is the author of *The Top Five Regrets of the Dying: A Life Transformed by the Dearly Departing*.

Bronnie found that many of the people she spoke to at the end of their lives recognized that, for much of their lives, they had stayed stuck in old patterns and habits. And they regretted it. She says 'The so-called "comfort" of familiarity overflowed into their ... lives. Fear of change had them pretending to others, and to themselves, that they were content.'

## Popular misconception

We often feel the pressure to make the 'right' decision and that makes it even harder to admit later we feel differently. Politicians usually face a great deal of scorn when they change their minds about an issue. Their opponents accuse them of making a U-turn and declare them to be inconsistent, weak and unreliable. This sends a message to the rest of us that changing your mind is a negative thing; it suggests weakness and a lack of confidence.

Not so!

All that's happened is that you feel differently about it now. That's ok. You're allowed to change your mind! Rather than feeling bad about having changed your mind about something, feel good. Simply see yourself as having made a new decision.

## SEVEN WAYS TO THINK DIFFERENTLY ABOUT THINKING DIFFERENTLY

1. Realize that at the time, based on what you knew and how you felt, you made the right choice. At the time, your decision was the right one. That was then. Now though, the situation isn't right for you. Accept that.

2. Think about how you will feel by letting go. Relieved? Pleased? Overjoyed? Although it will take time for you to adjust, you will have less anxiety and stress and more control over your life.

3. If you are thinking about the sunk costs – the time, effort, love or money you have already put in – accept that they are in the past and that you can never get those things back. There's no need to continue putting more time, effort or money into someone or something that's plainly not doing you any good.

4. Remind yourself that refusing to let go of something that's making you miserable means you are allowing the past to dictate the present.

5. Find something positive about the situation you've been stuck in. You can always draw something good out.

6. Think about what you have learned from the experience – what you have learned about yourself and anyone or anything else – that is helpful for you to know from now on.

7. Acknowledge what you have to lose by letting go, but then focus your mind on what you have to gain from the moment you let go. What will letting go then free you up to do? Know that all that matters is which option will be the best from this moment forward.

*'If you can change your mind you can change your life.'*

William James

## Moving forward

Think through your options. If you can't see an alternative way forward, get some support, advice and information from friends, family or colleagues. Ask for their ideas. Seek professional advice if you need information from an expert.

If someone else is going to be disappointed as a result of you changing your mind – if for example, you are going to stop going to a regular event with someone – tell them as soon as you can. Give one reason, not lots of excuses. Say what, if anything, you can do to compensate or help them adjust. For example; 'I'm not going to the running club any more. Maybe someone else can give you a lift each Tuesday?'

Other people *will* adjust; they can and will sort it out. But if you stay in that situation you'll feel trapped and unhappy – stuck in a situation you don't like and unable to get on with what you want to do from now on.

## Having courage

In an interview with Tami Simon for the podcast *Insights at the Edge,* palliative care nurse Bronnie Ware explains that what she learned from her patients about their regrets had a profound effect on her own life. 'All of the regrets really came down to a lack of courage, so having witnessed the anguish of regrets .... and realizing the sacredness of our time, I've been able to live a life true to myself now, and that meant letting go of doing jobs that didn't suit me because I thought that was what I had to do.'

Bronnie says that now, all her decisions are informed by asking herself, 'OK, if I don't do this, I'm going to regret it or I'm not? Which way am I going to go? I'm going to go the way that causes the least regret, even if it's the scariest way or the most challenging way.'

Bronnie believes it all comes down to courage. 'It's as simple and as difficult as that ... so much of everyone's lives – initially, until they make that choice to start the healing and truly honour the life that they are called to live, that we're all called to live – is shaped by courage, or is shaped by fear.'

Having courage doesn't mean not being afraid. Courage means doing something even though you are afraid and you know there are going to be difficulties and problems extricating yourself from a situation.

Whether it's leaving your job, a course or a relationship or moving home, courage is what makes you brave and helps you move forward in spite of your fears and concerns. Courage can also help you do what you want to do in spite of other people's fears or concerns, their objections or disapproval.

## How to draw on your courage to help you let go and move forward

- **Focus on the positive:** Remind yourself why you want to do something. What do you stand to gain? This can give you the motivation and courage you need to take the necessary first step.
- **Rather than fight feelings of fear and doubt, acknowledge and accept them:** Tell yourself: 'I'm feeling scared. I'm not sure about this.' Then push past those thoughts and feelings and tell yourself: 'But I *can* do this.' Feel the fear. And then do it.
- **Identify the steps you'll take:** Whatever it is that you need to do – to ditch the job, leave the course or let go of the friendship – breaking it down into smaller more doable steps can help make it far less daunting. Once you've taken the first step you'll have got things started and you can deal with it from there.
- **Focus on the first step:** Having thought through the steps, now just focus on that first step. Write that letter. Send the email. Fill in the form. Make the appointment. Make that first phone call. Talk to the other person. Say: 'I have something to tell you.' Get legal advice. Once you start doing something, it's easier to continue doing it. Take action and things will flow from there. That's why it helps to have a plan for the steps you need to take; it's easier if you know what you're doing first and what step comes next. Keep your mind focused on one step at a time. Tell yourself: 'This is what I'm going to do now' and then just focus on that one step you're taking. Then take the next step and you see yourself coping and moving forward.
- **Make it happen now:** You don't have to wait to feel confident and fearless before you get going. Get going and you'll just be getting on with it.

- **Get things in perspective:** Understand that whatever it is you have to let go of and walk away from, as difficult to manage as it is, days and weeks, or months and years from now, it will be just something you had to deal with before you could change course and be free to do what makes you happy. Getting things into perspective helps you to recognize that whether you take action or not, life will continue. So you might as well take action and make things work out so that as life continues, it does so in the ways you want it to.

## Exercise: Be inspired

- Inspire yourself. Think of a situation in the past when you felt afraid, yet faced your fear and took action. In your journal, describe the situation, what happened and how you felt at the time. What helped you let go? What was it that made you take that bold step?
- Be inspired by other people. Talk to others about what changes they made in their lives – what they had to change, let go of etc. – in order to be happy. Ask them if they were anxious or scared, how did they deal with it? How did things turn out for them?

## Affirmations

If you are stuck in a situation that you want to let go of, choosing one or two affirmations to repeat to yourself, can encourage you:

- Past decisions do not need to dictate what I do from now on.
- I am leaving the past in the past.
- I can leave behind the old ways of doing and being and welcome the new ones.
- I move on to a new chapter in my life.
- What happens and what I do from now on is all that matters.

# Key points

- Too often, instead of letting go of something that we're not enjoying, we feel we 'should' keep going, that we 'ought' to stick with it. Despite being unhappy, we continue to remain with something or someone.

- For a number of reasons, it's not always easy to detach ourselves, let go and move on to better things. It's not easy. But it's not impossible. Remind yourself that refusing to let go of something that's making you miserable means you are allowing the past to dictate the present. Leave past decisions behind you; think about what's best for you from now on. And begin again.

- **Set yourself an intention**: Be courageous. Feel the fear. And then do it. Acknowledge then push past feelings of fear and doubt. Get support and information, plan the steps, focus on the first step and tell yourself: 'I *can* do this.'

# Day 11

## AIM
To accept that all things will pass.

## THOUGHT FOR TODAY
*They are not long, the weeping and the laughter,*
*Love and desire and hate:*
*I think they have no portion in us after*
*We pass the gate.*
*They are not long, the days of wine and roses:*
*Out of a misty dream*
*Our path emerges for a while, then closes*
*Within a dream.*

*Ernest Dowson*

Ernest Dowson's poem describes how all things pass. Weeping and laughter, love, desire and hate, he says, do not last long. And neither do the days of pleasure and happiness, which he describes as 'the days of wine and roses'.

Everything that comes into this world also leaves it. Just as the seasons come and go, so does night and day, sun and rain, health and wealth, war and peace. Nothing is permanent and all eventually ends.

Mindfulness encourages us to understand, accept and embrace the concept of impermanence; to understand that whether it's weeping or laughter, pain or pleasure, it *will* pass. Difficulties and problems aren't permanent. One way or another, they will pass. Enjoyment and pleasure also pass. Mindfulness can help you to understand this; to appreciate the good, the enjoyable and happy times, to make the most of now, knowing it will not last.

## Exercise: Melting ice cube meditation

Put an ice cube on a plate. Then take a minute to be still and centre yourself, bringing your attention to your breathing as it comes in and out. After a minute or so, place the ice cube on the palm of your hand.

- Feel the texture of the ice. Watch the ice melt and the water drip through your fingers.
- Be aware of your thoughts, your physical sensations, and any emotional response you have.
- Do you feel a stinging sensation? Burning, or tingling?
- Notice what's going through your mind. Maybe you're thinking of how long you'll need to wait it out until the cube melts. Are you're hoping it will end soon?

The ice cube meditation can help you recognize and accept the impermanence of mental and physical discomfort. It can also help you recognize that railing against it only serves to exacerbate the discomfort.

## Exercise: Hand squeezing meditation

If you don't have an ice cube, try the following meditation:

- Make tight fists with both of your hands. Breathe in for about ten seconds and tighten your hands as you breathe in.
- Squeeze tighter. Squeeze till it hurts.
- Breathe out and release your hands. Now focus on how your hands feel and stay focused for as long as you can or until that feeling goes away.

The hand squeezing meditation can also help you recognize the impermanence of mental and physical discomfort and your emotional response to it.

## Exercise: Household activities

In your journal write down which of the following activities you dislike doing. Add any other household activities you can think of that you dislike:

- cooking
- washing up
- loading/unloading the dishwasher
- laundry
- food shopping
- changing bed linen
- cleaning windows
- mowing the lawn
- decorating
- vacuuming
- cleaning the loo
- taking the rubbish out
- cleaning out pets' cages/litter trays

What are your thoughts when you are doing any of the activities you dislike? Are they thoughts of impatience, irritation and frustration?

When you give meaning to these activities, and judge them as onerous or annoying and begrudge doing them, you turn them into unpleasant difficulties and irritations. Even using the words 'chores' and 'tasks' to describe these activities conceptualizes them as inherently unpleasant.

It's not the activity itself, but your thoughts about it, that creates the pain.

Mindfulness involves accepting a situation as it is, not as your mind judges it. Washing up is just washing up. Cleaning windows is just cleaning windows. Cleaning the loo is just cleaning the loo. And so on. These activities only become chores – unpleasant tasks – if you think of them in that way. You only need to do the job. It will pass. Once you've done it, it's passed. Until the next time. And then you do it again. And it passes. And so on.

## Attachment

According to Buddhism, attachment is the root of suffering. When you identify with and rail against something you attach yourself to it; the activity, the dislike and yourself are as one. But understanding that the task and your dislike are separate from you can help you accept that it is what it is. Neither good nor bad. Just an activity to carry out. And that it will pass.

## Meditation: A place to practise acceptance

When you practise a focused-awareness meditation you also practise acceptance. As you focus on your breathing, each time a thought enters your head, rather than get frustrated, you simply accept you've lost focus. You let the thought pass and you return your attention to your breathing. And in an 'open monitoring' meditation you accept your thoughts as just thoughts.

In this way, meditation can help you develop acceptance for everyday occurrences. So, in today's example of housework, meditation and a mindful attitude helps train your mind to be more able to accept housework as just housework. You learn not to make it a 'thing' by disliking it and then railing against it. You carry out the activity, you complete it and it has passed.

## Gaining a sense of perspective

*'Perspective is everything when you are experiencing the challenges of life.'*

Joni Eareckson Tada

When a problem or challenge happens in your life, when the difficulties are relentless and it feels that they'll never end, gaining perspective can help. Gaining perspective means getting a sense of where you are in the greater scheme of things; taking everything else into account.

If, for example, you fail an exam, perspective helps you to understand that, as difficult to manage as it is right now, the situation *will* change. Life will continue and one way or another, things *will* work out.

A sense of perspective often makes the difference between resisting or accepting unwanted change and difficulties when they happen in your life. Perspective can give you a state of calm where, right now, you can rest without needing things to be different. This doesn't mean that you have to resign yourself to something. You don't have to give in. It means accepting and understanding that at this moment, something is what it is.

You might want for things to be different in the future, but in the present moment you accept things as they are and for what they are, knowing that this too *will* pass.

## Exercise: Getting things into perspective

Try the following to bring perspective into your current situation:

- **Ask someone over the age of 70 about their life:** What went well and what didn't? Have they experienced fear, sadness and struggle? How did things turn out for them? How do they now view some of those problems when viewed in relation to everything else that happened in their life? Be aware that right now you are the one living the life you will speak of when you are older.
- **Think of your own experiences:** Have you had an experience that was a setback, a challenge or a problem to deal with? What happened? Was the problem resolved? How did it pass? However long it lasted, it wasn't permanent. One way or another it passed. Things may not have worked out the way you wanted them to, but they didn't remain the same. Things moved on. Remind yourself of this when you're in the middle of a difficult, challenging experience. Remind yourself: 'This too shall pass.'
- **Read about other people's lives:** *Water for Elephants* by Sara Gruen is a partial narrative by a 93-year-old man looking back at his days in the circus during the Great Depression. *Tuesdays with Morrie* by Mitch Albom tells the true story of a man who looks up his former university professor and listens to stories about his life.

# Acknowledging and appreciating good times

*'Let everything happen to you. Beauty and terror. Just keep going. No feeling is final.'*

*Rainer Maria Rilke*

Just as suffering, problems and difficulties will not last, neither do enjoyment and pleasure. Mindfulness can help you to understand this; to appreciate the good, the enjoyable and happy times, to make the most of now, knowing it will not last. The chocolate meditation and music meditation are examples of this.

## Exercise: Chocolate meditation

- Break off a square of chocolate and place it in your mouth.
- Allow it to slowly melt into the warmth of your mouth.
- Reflect on and enjoy the flavour and texture of the chocolate.
- Be aware of how the chocolate gradually melts away until it is no longer there.

## Exercise: Music meditation

Choose a favourite piece of music or a song to listen to. Play it on whatever device is convenient right now. Do nothing else but listen to the music. Enjoy it. Be aware of the pleasure you are experiencing. Close your eyes and listen to how sounds appear and disappear, as does the piece of music itself.

# Sound baths

A sound bath is a unique way to experience the concept of impermanence. A sound bath is a meditative practice where you experience being bathed in sound waves. These waves are produced by instruments such as gongs, singing bowls, chimes and bells. Allowing yourself to completely tune in to the sounds creates a shift of mind allowing you to disconnect your mind from your thoughts by entering into a meditative state.

The sounds and the harmonies come and they go.

You don't have to do anything except listen. The sounds wash over you, leading you into a state of calm and relaxation. You simply give yourself up to the sounds as they come and they go.

Go to www.collegeofsoundhealing.co.uk to find out about sound bath sessions taking place near you. You will also be able to find sound bath apps online and sound bath videos on YouTube.

# Affirmations

Affirmations can be harbingers of change. Whether it's weeping or laughter, pain or pleasure, an affirmation that you have memorized can remind you that it *will* pass:

- This may be difficult, but it *will* pass.
- One way or another, things *will* work out.
- This too, *will* pass.
- I'm aware of and appreciate the good times, knowing they *will* pass.
- Appreciate the good, the enjoyable and happy times, to make the most of now, knowing it *will not* last.

# Key points

- Everything that comes into this world also leaves it. Just as the seasons come and go, so does night and day, sun and rain, health and wealth, war and peace. Nothing is permanent and all eventually ends.

- When you give meaning to activities and experiences, judge them as annoying, begrudge and resent them, not only do your thoughts about them create difficulty and discomfort, but those thoughts get in the way of recognizing that whatever the experience or activity, it will pass.

- Mindfulness encourages us to understand, accept and embrace the concept of impermanence; to understand that difficulties and problems aren't permanent. One way or another, they will pass. Enjoyment and pleasure also passes. Mindfulness can help you to understand this; to appreciate the good, the enjoyable and happy times, to make the most of now, knowing it will not last.

- **Set yourself an intention:** Today, raise your awareness; be aware of the impermanence of things; objects, experiences and feelings, the people in your life. Reflect on the things in your life that have come and then gone.

# Day 12

## AIM
To think with a beginner's mind.

## THOUGHT FOR TODAY
*'Be willing to be a beginner every single morning.'*

*Meister Eckhart*

Today, before you read any further, start with a simple two-minute focused-attention meditation. Each time you are aware that a thought has come into your mind, let it go and return your attention to your breathing.

With a focused-attention meditation, each time you return your attention to your breathing, you are beginning again. Each time you lose focus, you just begin again. There's no need to be disappointed, irritated or annoyed if your mind wanders. Just return to your breathing. Begin again. Have a beginner's mind.

Beginner's mind is a mindfulness concept that suggests that everything can and does begin again, in the present moment.

During meditation, a beginner's mind allows you to detach and move on from unhelpful thoughts. In your everyday life, beginner's mind also frees you from unhelpful thoughts. You detach yourself from assumptions, expectations and preconceived ideas and conclusions about yourself, other people, events and situations. And you begin again.

Rather than respond to events, experiences, places and other people in the same old ways – ways from the past – beginner's mind encourages you to start again; to take a new perspective and to respond to things as they are right now, in the present.

## The tale of the overflowing teacup

A student comes to a Zen master and asks for instruction in the way of Zen Buddhism.

The master begins to explain that Zen emphasizes the value of meditation and intuition rather than ritual worship or study of scripture. In an attempt to impress him the student interrupts the master and says, 'Oh, I already know that.'

The master then invites the student to have some tea. When the tea is ready, the master pours the tea into a teacup, filling it to the brim, spilling tea over the sides of the cup and onto the table.

The student exclaims, 'Stop! You can't pour tea into a full cup.'

The master replies, 'Return to me when your cup is empty.'

The moral of the story is, of course, that a beginner's mind is empty. It holds no preconceived ideas about what is or what isn't. It is open and receptive to the possibility of new ideas and new ways.

Usually, what we do and how we think is based on what we think we already know. We think about ourselves, other people, places and the world in the same way as we've always thought about them and we do things in the same way that we always have.

But responding to other people, situations and events in familiar, established ways limits how we receive and respond to the world around us. It makes it likely that we'll miss out on all sorts of possibilities and discoveries, new ideas and ways of seeing and understanding.

## Exercise: Identifying mind traps

It's easy to become trapped in a single understanding – to be unaware that what we believe and how we think is based on past thoughts and experience. Typically, it doesn't occur to us that there might be another way to think. Which of these mind traps do you sometimes fall into?

- **The confirmation trap:** this occurs when you only believe information that supports what you already believe. The confirmation trap is also the basis for prejudice; pre-judging a situation or person based on what you think you know and believe to be true.
- **Jumping to conclusions:** when you jump to a conclusion, you decide on something before you have all the relevant information or evidence.
- **Tunnel thinking:** with tunnel thinking, in any one situation, your mind excludes possibilities and options; there is only one direction for your thoughts; they see only one outcome.
- **The conformity trap:** when you fall into the conformity trap, you fall in with other people's way of thinking. You go along with and agree with their thoughts, ideas and perspectives. You fail to consider other views and perspectives.

In your journal, briefly describe a situation where you have fallen into one or more of these mind traps.

## Being aware of thoughts

On Day 3 you read that for meditation – or any other activity – to become a habit, you have to do it regularly. Quite simply, the more often you do something the more likely it will become a habit. That's because each time you do or think about something in a particular way, you strengthen the 'neural pathways' in your brain; you strengthen that way of doing or thinking so that it becomes habitual.

There are positive and negative aspects to this. The positive aspect is that you can then do things and think about things automatically and quickly. You are, for example, in the habit of looking both ways when you cross the road. You are also in the habit of brushing your teeth each evening. You don't have to remind yourself to do this. You do it automatically.

The negative aspect of the habitual ways of thinking and doing is the fact that we no longer do things or think about things differently. Our brains revert to familiar ways of 'seeing' and understanding. When it assumes it knows what it's seeing, or being asked to do, it stops looking for further possibilities. And that's not always a good thing; your mind can get trapped in unhelpful thoughts.

Mind traps and habitual ways of thinking are so powerful *because* you rarely have conscious awareness of them. More often than not, you won't even notice when you're thinking in the same way you have always done. It's a habit to think that way.

But with a beginner's mind, you are aware that there's more than one way of thinking and behaving. With a beginner's mind you consciously put aside beliefs, judgements and conclusions you have that are based on past ways of thinking and doing. You know that each time you let go of the thoughts of how things 'should' or 'shouldn't' be, 'must' or 'musn't' be. You free yourself to think in new ways. To begin again.

The more often you approach life with a beginner's mind, the more often you get to experience life in the present moment.

## You already have a beginner's mind

The good news is that you've already been practising a beginner's mind. Since Day 1 you've been encouraged to be accepting. Over the last few days, you will have learned that when you accept that nothing can change what has or hasn't already happened, you free your mind to move forward in positive, more helpful ways. You begin again.

Acceptance creates space for new beginnings: letting go, letting things pass and recognizing that all things *will* pass teaches us that there are always new beginnings.

---

## Exercise: Positive thinking

There are a number of ways that you can continue to practise beginner's mind. Here are two suggestions.

- Think of someone you have always found difficult to get on with, for example, a family member or a colleague. Think about what irritates, upsets or annoys you about them. You may want to write about this in your journal. Now, put aside your beliefs and opinions and see something new about them. Look for something positive. It could be an aspect of their personality, their attitude, something about the way they interact with others an ability or a skill they have. In your journal, describe the positive aspects you have identified. Know that by doing this – by looking for something positive in someone else – you are seeing them with a beginner's mind.
- Go back to the household activities you identified in Day 11 as chores you dislike doing. As well as accepting that an activity only has meaning if you give it any meaning, you can also change the meaning you give it. Begin again; give the activities a positive meaning. For example, vacuuming and cleaning windows can be thought of as a way of doing physical exercise. Washing up and ironing can be seen as an opportunity to listen to music or a podcast. Or an opportunity for some mindful breathing.

---

### SEVEN GOOD REASONS TO HAVE BEGINNER'S MIND
A beginner's mind is an open mind. A beginner's mind helps you:

1. **Be more aware:** Challenging your existing beliefs and considering new ideas can give you new perspectives, and positive, fresh insights about yourself, other people and the world around you.

2. **Have new experiences**: Being open to new ways of thinking about things can also open you up to new ideas, opportunities, experiences and ways of doing things.

3. **Empathize**: Being open to other people's situations helps you to be more understanding and able to empathize and have compassion for others.

4. **Adapt to changes in your life**: A beginner's mind makes it more likely that you can adapt to changes when they occur in your life. Just as we all had to adapt to the changes in our lives that happened during the COVID-19 pandemic.

5. **Learn new things**: A beginner's mind is a learner's mind. And a learner's mind is a beginner's mind.

6. **Accept and let go**: A beginner's mind allows you to accept and move on from past mistakes, difficulties and failures and begin again, as with a fresh new page.

7. **Enjoy life more**: When you don't have assumptions, beliefs and expectations, you are less likely to be disappointed or frustrated by an experience, because there's no preconceived idea to compare it to.

## Five ways to keep an open mind

1. Talk to someone with a different perspective, occupation, background, culture or religion. Read or watch programmes about people who are different from you. This will increase the odds that you're introduced to new ways of thinking.

2. Seek out opposing viewpoints. Be aware that consuming news from the same news outlets and social media feeds just strengthens what you already believe. To avoid falling into mind traps – confirmation traps and conformity traps – decide what you think about an issue then seek out alternative perspectives.

3. Volunteer your time to help people in situations that are completely different from your own. Meet new people. New people bring new thoughts, ideas and perceptions into your life.

4. Got a problem or difficulty and not sure how to manage or solve it? Think about how someone else you know – someone

in a different position – would think about it or solve it. Ask them for their ideas and insight.

5. Whenever you are aware of having an opinion or view about yourself, someone else, an event or an issue, add the word 'but'. This forces you to think differently. For example, 'I think he's brought his misfortune on himself. *But* ... ' The word 'but' leads to a new way to think about it.

## Affirmations

Choose one or more of the affirmations below, and in your journal write it out three times:

- The present is always an opportunity to begin again.
- Each time I let go of the thoughts of how things 'should' be and accept something as it is, I begin again.
- There is more than one way to think of this. What is it?
- With a beginner's mind there are many possibilities.

# Key points

- Beginner's mind suggests that everything can and does begin again, in the present moment. Rather than respond to events, experiences, places and other people in the same old ways – ways from the past – beginner's mind encourages you to start again; to take a new perspective and to respond to things as they are right now, in the present.

- Beginner's mind enables you to be more aware and accepting. Challenging your existing beliefs and considering new ideas can give you new perspectives, positive, fresh insights about yourself, other people and the world around you.

- **Set yourself an intention:** Today, do the two positive thinking exercises. And from now on, remind yourself to keep an open mind. Choose one or two affirmations to memorize and to tell yourself.

# Day 13

**AIM**
To act with a beginner's mind.

**THOUGHT FOR TODAY**
*There is an abundance of opportunities to do new things and do familiar things differently.*

Rather than respond to events, experiences, places and other people in the same old ways – ways from the past – beginner's mind encourages you to think about and respond to yourself and other people, events and experiences around you as they are right now, in the present.

As well as thinking in new ways, you can also develop a beginner's mind by:

- being aware of new things in familiar situations
- doing familiar things in unfamiliar ways
- learning something new
- doing something for the first time

Making a point of noticing something new in familiar situations, doing familiar things differently, learning something new and doing something you've never done before puts you in the present. Why? Because when things are new and different, your awareness is heightened; you are more aware of what's happening right here, right now.

---

### Exercise: Look for what's new

Today, on your way to and from work, the school run or walking your dog, set an intention to look for changes in the environment. Look for what – compared to the last time you took this route – is new and different. Is it the same in every way as the same journey last time? What's different? If you resolve to be more aware you'll see that almost everything is different each time: the weather, the sky, the pattern of light on the buildings, the people you pass.

When you walk into your home, place of work or a shop, what do you notice? What do you see, hear or smell that is different?

In your journal, describe what new things you noticed in these familiar situations.

---

# The same, but always different

Some years ago, while driving a route he regularly took past a huge oak tree in south-west Wisconsin, photographer Mark Hirsch stopped his truck on the country road he was driving down, to take a photo of the burr oak tree. Mark then decided to make it a project; he took a new photo of the tree every day for almost a year. (Go to www.thattree.net/ to see the photos.)

You could do the same as Mark Hirsch. Whether you are outside in an open space, in a town or city or simply looking at something outside your window at home or work, even though you may have looked at it many times before, regularly taking a photo of something can be like seeing it for the first time and can help you see the world around you differently or, simply, for what it is.

## Exercise: Make yourself aware of the unfamiliar in the familiar

- **Listen to music as if for the first time:** With a beginner's mind you can listen to familiar pieces of music as if for the first time. Choose a favourite piece of music. Pick out an element that you don't usually listen to – the beat, the melody, the lyrics or a particular instrument. Now listen to and follow the music, focusing on the new element you have chosen. Even though you might have listened to this music many times before, when you listen with a beginner's mind, you experience it anew. You are in the moment.
- **Appreciate the things you own as if for the first time:** After the initial thrill of buying something – lovely new shoes, a new faster computer, a smartphone, a fab new sofa – the excitement wears off. This is because you get used to it. A beginner's mind encourages you to appreciate the things you already own, as if for the first time. Choose three things that you own – an object, piece of clothing, a book, an ornament, a piece of furniture, a piece of equipment, a bike or car. In your journal, describe the benefits and pleasures that each of those three things give you.

# Doing familiar things in unfamiliar ways

As well as being aware of when familiar things are different, making a point of doing familiar things in unfamiliar ways – changing even small routines – is a good way of practising beginner's mind: to think in new ways and to be open to new possibilities.

---

### Exercise: Routine activities

In your journal, note down which of these activities you usually do at the same time every day.

- get up
- eat breakfast
- go for a run or to the gym
- eat lunch and dinner
- walk the dog
- go to bed
- have a shower or bath

Which of these activities are usually the same and unchanging?

- what you eat for breakfast each morning
- the route you take to work/to visit friends and family
- the supermarket you shop at
- the route you walk round the supermarket

---

Doing things in the same ways at the same times means that you don't have to think about what you're doing. Of course this is helpful; routines are a shortcut to avoid having to think things through every time. The things you do on a regular basis – the route you take to work or to visit friends and family, for example – you are so used to doing you don't have to think about doing them. But in a range of situations, you miss so much when you do familiar things in the same old ways. You become mindless instead of mindful.

Beginner's mind doesn't suggest making changes for the sake of change. It doesn't suggest that you fix something that isn't broke. Beginner's mind also doesn't dismiss or devalue how you do something or the way you've usually done things. It simply suggests you be more aware of when you are doing something in the same old way; that now and then, you are open to doing things differently.

## Exercise: Do familiar things differently with a beginner's mind

Choosing to break a routine way of doing things on a regular basis can be an effective way to kickstart new ways of thinking, seeing and understanding. Even small changes can help. Try the following:

- **Take a different route:** Is there a journey you take on a regular basis; to work, to school, to visit family and friends? Try leaving a little bit earlier and take a different route.
- **Walk a different way round the supermarket:** If you have a route that you normally take around the supermarket aisles, change the route.
- **Change your mode of travel:** Walk instead of cycle. Cycle instead of drive. Or get public transport. Take the stairs instead of the lift.
- **Change where you sit:** At work, sit in a different seat in meetings or where you sit for lunch. If you use public transport, sit somewhere different from where you normally sit on the bus or train.

### THREE GOOD REASONS TO NOTICE THE NEW IN THE FAMILIAR

1. Noticing new things in familiar situations and actively seeking out new ways to do routine activities is putting mindful, intentional living into practice. You are more aware and you acknowledge what's happening right now; you are experiencing life in the present moment.

2. You slow down. Noticing new things and doing things differently slows you down. And that can be a good thing! If you're often rushing from one thing to the next, taking the time to be more aware is a good way to slow down. The change in pace allows you to be more calm. (More about this on Day 16.)

3. You are more curious about yourself, other people and the world. Life is more interesting!

*'The real voyage of discovery consists not in seeking new landscapes, but in having new eyes.'*

*Marcel Proust*

## Exercise: Doing something new

As well as noticing something new in familiar situations, or doing familiar things differently, learning something new, and taking part in new activities and experiences, is the definitive way of having a beginner's mind – because you really are starting at the beginning.

When was the last time you did something for the first time? When did you last learn something new?

In your journal, describe a time you did something new. Then, choose to do one of the following activities. After you have done the activity, write in your journal. What was it like? What did you learn?

- Visit a place that you haven't explored before. Walk around a part of your town that you've never been to, or take a country walk on footpaths you've not walked before.
- Get lost. Trust your internal compass and wend your way around somewhere new. You never know where and what you might discover! Getting lost can be an interesting experience; finding your way back, you're more aware; your senses are sharpened, you see more and remember more.
- Try some new food or cook a new dish for dinner.
- Read a book, watch a film or a TV series that you know nothing about; you've not read any reviews or heard anyone talk

about it. Listen to new music or a different radio station from what you would normally choose.

- Do something brave: Go on a roller coaster, watch a horror movie, hold a spider. If you usually eat out with other people, go on your own. Or go and see a film by yourself.
- Try a new activity; a dance class, yoga or tennis. Try canoeing or paddle boarding.
- Learn something new. It could simply be a new recipe but it could be a new skill – to play the piano, learn a language, creative writing, bricklaying or drawing. It could be a sport – tennis or badminton. Find something you have never done before.

## Feeling the fear and doing it anyway

In an interview with the *Guardian* newspaper in 2018, Jacqueline Thomas, 52, described how, three years earlier, she'd moved to a village with her partner David. They didn't know anyone in the area so had to start getting to know other people from scratch. The variety of classes and groups that Jacqueline signed up for at the village hall was the start of some new friendships.

Jacqueline, who is a wheelchair user, signed up for something that was completely new for her; an adapted martial arts class. She was surprised to find how much she enjoyed it. Encouraged by her teacher, Carl Hodgetts, who in 2006 became the first wheelchair-using kickboxing instructor in the UK, she went on to achieve a white belt in Shiying Do adapted martial art. Jacqueline says that joining in with something that's new to you just takes one leap of faith. 'Even if you're absolutely terrified, do it,' she says, adding, 'Even I'm a bit shocked about the martial arts, though.' Jacqueline's advice is, 'Don't be afraid of being scared. Do it anyway.'

Like Jacqueline, Jessica Pan author of *Sorry I'm Late, I Didn't Want to Come: An Introvert's Year of Living Dangerously*, also tried something new. In an interview with BBC Radio 4's *Woman's Hour*, Jessica described how, in her year of trying out new activities and experiences, she took classes that scared her: 'When I did a comedy course I met amazing friends, and on the improv course I met creative people that I would never have met otherwise.'

**THREE GOOD REASONS TO DO SOMETHING FOR THE FIRST TIME**

1. When you are learning and doing things for the first time you pay more attention which means that these new activities are intrinsically mindful.
2. Being open to new ways of thinking about things can also open you up to new opportunities, experiences and ways of doing things.
3. You are better able to adapt when changes are forced upon you.

## Affirmations

- Be now, not then.
- There's always something new to notice.
- It's never too late to do something new.
- I unlock new possibilities by being open to doing new things.
- Anything can start here and now.

DAY 13

# Key points

- Making a point of noticing something new in familiar situations, doing familiar things differently, learning something new and doing something you've never done before can help you develop a beginner's mind.

- Noticing new things in familiar situations and actively seeking out new ways to do routine activities is putting mindful, intentional living into practice; you are more aware, able to acknowledge and be accepting of what's happening right here, right now.

- **Set yourself an intention:** Today, do one thing differently. Look for something new in a familiar situation. Do one thing you've never done before.

# Day 14

## AIM
To understand the positive intentions of emotions.

## THOUGHT FOR TODAY
*All emotions have a positive purpose.*

In a range of situations, a beginner's mind not only allows you to think and behave differently, but also to respond differently; to respond to emotions differently.

On Day 6 you were encouraged to be aware of and acknowledge the specific situations that trigger strong, difficult emotions. Then, in any one situation, rather than be overcome by an emotion, resist or deny how you are feeling, you can take a step back, acknowledge and accept that you are angry for example, or that you are frustrated or that you are feeling very disappointed or feeling guilty. And that's ok!

Rather than feed an emotion – telling yourself how bad or unfair the situation is, or that someone else 'made' you feel this way – accepting the emotion and how you feel frees your mind to tune in to the message that the emotion is communicating.

We often think of emotions as being either positive or negative. Emotions such as happiness, hope and joy, for example, we think of as being positive, but emotions such as resentment, impatience, shame and jealousy we think of as being negative.

The fact is, all emotions have a positive purpose. Emotions such as fear, anger, sadness and regret might not feel good – they are uncomfortable, and often painful feelings – but they do have a beneficial purpose. They're prompting you to take positive, helpful action in response to something that has happened, is happening or could happen.

When you touch something that's very hot, the physical pain prompts you to respond positively, to move your hand away. Emotional pain is the same; it prompts you to respond positively.

The problem is, when we experience a 'negative' emotion, we often react in ways that make a situation worse. We either allow the emotion to overwhelm us or we deny or get stuck in the emotion. But reactions like these just prolong our pain and suffering.

Take, for example, regret. Regret is a feeling of sorrow and loss that occurs when you wish that you had or had not done something. The positive intent of regret is to prompt you to pause and reflect on your mistake and decide how to avoid making a similar mistake in future; to move on and begin again. Regret is only negative if you become stuck in negative thoughts, self-blame and inaction. It's not the emotion that's negative, it's you berating yourself instead of calmly and compassionately reflecting and learning from your mistake.

**DID YOU KNOW?**

What do you think might be the positive purpose of the following two emotions?

**Sadness** is the internalized expression of emotion characterized by feelings of loss and helplessness.

The positive intent of sadness is to help you slow down, so that you can take in and accept whatever it is that has happened; to adjust to loss and move on from there. Sadness becomes a problem if you are unable to accept what has happened and you become trapped in a downward spiral of apathy, disinterest and pessimism that can lead to bitterness, despair and depression.

**Anger** is the strong feeling, the sense of injustice, that you or someone else has been wronged, offended, threatened or attacked in some way.

The positive intent of anger is to prompt you to take control and put right a wrongdoing. If it's justified and expressed appropriately it can be a legitimate way to change a situation for the better. But it can just as easily be destructive and do more harm than good. Often, we either try to suppress or deny our anger or we give full vent to our anger.

Try to keep in mind that emotions serve a positive purpose. Emotions are your mind and body's way of communicating with you. They're trying to get you to take positive, helpful action in response to something that has happened, is happening or could happen.

## How to identify the positive intention of an emotion

How might you know what the positive purpose of an emotion is? Generally, the answer can be found in the definition – the meaning – of the emotion. Here are some examples.

**Guilt:**

**The emotion:** guilt is the feeling of responsibility or remorse for some offence or wrongdoing that you believe you've committed.

**The positive intention:** to prompt you to put right your wrongdoing.
**Envy:**
**The emotion:** envy is feeling resentful because someone else has something you want but don't have.

**The positive intention:** to motivate you to acquire what the other person has, that you want.
**Disgust:**
**The emotion:** disgust is a strong aversion – a feeling of revulsion, nausea or loathing – about something or someone.

**The positive intention:** to prompt you to avoid the object of your disgust.

Once you are aware, acknowledge and have accepted an emotion, how you respond comes from your understanding of the positive message the emotion is telling you. Of course, how you put right the wrong, how you acquire what the other person has and how you avoid the object of your disgust is subject to either positive, constructive action or negative action on your part!

## DID YOU KNOW?

In certain situations, do you ever think or say: 'I know I shouldn't feel like this but ... ?'

When you have a belief that you 'shouldn't' have a particular emotion, or try and ignore, deny or suppress it, you cut off the opportunity to understand what the emotion is trying to tell you. Instead, acknowledge and accept that you do feel however you feel. Listen to the positive message the emotion is telling you, then let the emotion pass or respond calmly and rationally.

# Managing disappointment, regret and guilt

*'Guilt is good for you, provided it lasts no longer than five minutes and it brings about a change in behaviour.'*

*Author unknown*

Disappointment, guilt and regret are emotions that are reactions to something that happened in the past.

Disappointment is the feeling of sadness that occurs when things haven't turned out the way you expected or hoped that they would. Guilt is feeling responsible or remorseful for some offence or wrong-doing that you believe you've committed. Regret is the feeling of sorrow and loss that occurs when you wish that you had or had not done something.

Disappointment, guilt and regret are rooted in sadness. They might not feel nice, but like all other emotions, they do have a positive purpose. The positive purpose is to slow you down and give you time to take in the loss, failure or mistake; to take time to acknowledge and accept that what has happened *has* happened. And that nothing can change that.

## Exercise: Managing disappointment, regret and guilt

Think back to a situation where you experienced a disappointment or something happened that you felt guilty or regretful about (or think about something you currently feel disappointment, regret or guilt for.) Maybe you were disappointed because an event got cancelled? Perhaps you felt guilty because you did something that upset someone else? Perhaps you did or didn't do something you later regretted? In your journal, write notes on the following:

- **What happened?** Describe what happened and how you responded.
- **What did you learn?** Learning from disappointment, guilt and regret involves reflecting on what happened, identifying what went wrong, and working out what, if anything, you might do now to lessen the chance of a similar event happening in the future. What did you learn about yourself or someone else? What would you now do differently? Start again with a beginner's mind: be open to new ideas and ways of

doing things. Rather than think, 'I should/shouldn't have', try saying, 'Next time I'll ...', or, 'It might help to ...', or, 'I could ...', or, 'Now I'm going to ...'

- **Have compassion.** Be kind to yourself; know that you did what you did with what you knew at the time. Think about what you would say to someone else in the same situation to make them feel better. In your journal, write down what you would say.

# Managing worry and anxiety

Worry and anxiety are emotions that are rooted in fear. They are uncomfortable, often painful emotions, but like all other emotions, they do have a positive purpose. The positive purpose of worry and anxiety is to alert you to potential difficulties and problems that may occur in an upcoming event or situation and prompt you to do something to lessen the chances of those difficulties from happening. Anxiety about an exam, for example, can motivate you to focus, to cut out all distractions and revise. Anxiety only becomes negative if it so overwhelms you that you're unable to think clearly enough to do the revision. Or if you ignore or suppress it and so avoid revising.

Worry and anxiety can pull you out of the present moment and into an unknown future, allowing unrelenting doubts and fears and negative possibilities to overwhelm your mind and paralyse you. You may feel that you've no control over what could happen; how events might turn out and whether or not you'll be able to cope if things do go wrong.

However, a mindful approach can help you focus on the present moment, rather than pre-living the future.

## Exercise: Managing worry and anxiety

Is there something that you are currently worried or anxious about? An interview, an exam, a work issue, a health issue maybe? Perhaps you are anxious about attending a social event.

- Acknowledge your concern. In your journal, acknowledge what exactly it is that you are worried about. For example, rather than say, 'I'm worried about the interview', explain what aspects you are worried about. Is it, for example, that you're worried you won't be able to answer questions the interviewer asks you? Are you worried that you won't know what questions to ask in return? Externalizing your thoughts, fears and worries about events by writing them down is a helpful way to empty your mind so that you are free to focus on the present.

- Observe your thoughts. When you are aware of troubling thoughts, concerns and worries, say to yourself: 'Here's the thought that I might fail my exam/I won't get the job/I won't know anyone at the party.'

- Look for solutions. Focus on what you can do, rather than aspects of the situation that are beyond your control. Find one small step you can take now, in the present moment. It might be talking to someone else about it in order to get information, advice or support. It might be putting something into place to minimize the chances of the cause of your worry from happening. Once you start doing something about the problem, you may feel less worried because you are thinking and acting in the present rather than projecting yourself into the future.

- Now turn to something else that you can do right now. Identify activities that you can turn to when you want to switch off from worrying; something that you can dip into for ten minutes or immerse yourself in for an hour. Something that keeps you focused and engaged, that brings your complete attention to the present experience.

## Meditation to manage emotions

By their very nature, emotions are transitory. They are quick short messages that motivate you to respond in a way that is helpful. Emergencies aside, you don't have to react immediately. A mindful approach encourages you to be present and open to the positive message the emotion is communicating to you.

Practising an 'open monitoring' meditation trains your mind to acknowledge and accept difficult thoughts and emotions. You can step back from the emotion and accompanying thoughts and look for the positive message the emotion is telling you.

And, when you are aware that someone else is feeling a strong emotion – whether or not it's directed at you – you can try and understand what the positive purpose of the emotion is. You don't have to step in, just observe.

## A reminder

Slow, focused breathing helps bring your heartrate back down. Simply count to three on the in-breath and count to five on each out-breath. Do this for a couple of minutes. Just having to think about counting as you breathe will help re-engage your logical thinking brain. Then you will be more able to tune in to the positive message the emotion is sending you, and respond calmly and rationally.

## Affirmations

Affirmations can help you manage uncomfortable and difficult emotions. They can help you be aware, acknowledge and accept how you are feeling. Affirmations can validate how you feel; confirm that it is ok to feel whatever it is that you are feeling. Each affirmation is like a 'note to self.' It's a statement of what's true for you, or what's possible for you.

Choose one or more of the affirmations below or make up your own. Simple affirmations work best because they're easy to remember and get right to the point.

- It's ok to feel this way.
- All emotions have a positive purpose.
- Stop. Listen to what the emotion is telling me.
- I'm not okay right now, and that's okay. I won't always feel this way.
- This too will pass.
- I don't need to feel better right away. I can accept that right now, this is how I feel.
- Even though I feel like this, I am okay.
- I am going to focus on my breathing until I know how best to respond.

# Key points

- It's easy to get caught up in our emotions and instead of allowing them to inform and direct us in positive ways, we allow them to overwhelm us and keep us in the past (as with regret and guilt) or push us into the future (as with anxiety and impatience). And keep us there.

- Emotions such as fear, anger, sadness and regret might be uncomfortable, painful feelings but they *do* have a beneficial purpose. They're prompting you to take positive, helpful action in response to something that has happened, is happening or could happen.

- **Set yourself an intention:** Continue to practise an 'open monitoring' meditation; it can help train you to step back from an emotion and look for the positive message the emotion is telling you.

# Day 15

**AIM**
To focus and engage with the present.

**THOUGHT FOR TODAY**
*Be here now.*

Like so many of us, you probably have busy stressful periods where everything seems to be piling up.

Whether it's at work, study or home, there's so much to do and think about. And even if you *are* making headway with what you're doing, you are often interrupted or are easily distracted. You feel anxious, frustrated and overwhelmed and you struggle to think clearly, to focus and engage with what you need to do.

In situations like this, mindfulness can help. It starts with acceptance.

Although you have a lot to do, rather than waste time and energy making the situation worse by telling yourself (and anyone else) how unfair, how wrong and how difficult things are, acceptance frees your mind to think about what you can do to minimize and manage the difficulties.

## Exercise: Managing busy periods one step at a time

Any time that you have lots to do and the pressure is on, the following steps can help you.

- **Breathe.** Take two or three minutes to stop and focus on breathing. Slow, focused breathing helps slow everything down. Simply count to three on the in breath and count to five on each out breath. Do this for a couple of minutes. Just having to focus on counting as you breathe can help calm and clear your mind so that you can engage the rationalizing, reasoning part of your brain.
- **Empty your mind.** For any busy period – whether that's right now, later today, tomorrow, or in the next few days – get it all out of your head and write it down. Write a list of everything you need to do or have to do.
- **Prioritize and plan the tasks.** Next, go through your list and decide what's urgent and what's important – what really needs to be done. Decide what you are going to do first and in what order you are going to do everything else. How is this

mindful? As the time management expert Alan Lakein has said, 'Planning is bringing the future into the present so that you can do something about it now.' It's easier to get straight on to the next thing if you have already planned what, when and how you are going to do it. It allows you to maintain a steady pace and keep the pace going.

- **Get started.** Start with the first task. Do that one thing. Give it your full attention. Once that one task is done, do the next thing. Give that your full attention too. Be deliberate and purposeful. Then move on to the next thing. And when that's completed, move on to the next thing. In this way, you're only thinking about what you're doing while you're doing it. You are working mindfully.
- **Reassure yourself.** As you continue with what you are doing, any time you start to feel anxious and stressed remind yourself, 'I have a plan. I can manage this.'

## Habit to develop

During busy, stressful periods, try to get some breathing space two or three times a day. Take a couple of minutes to stop and focus on breathing. Simply count to three on the in breath and count to five on each out breath.

Breaks give your mind space to digest, mentally process and assimilate what's happening internally and externally. You don't need to try and do it consciously. It's something that the brain just does naturally below the surface.

## Managing interruptions and distractions

Although planning and prioritizing the tasks and working through each task one step at a time can help you maintain a focused steady pace, it can easily be broken by interruptions and distractions.

Interruptions arrive unexpectedly at any time. Interruptions come from other people in the way of questions, announcements, requests and demands. They want decisions made, conflicts managed and problems solved.

A distraction can be anything that diverts your attention or that you allow yourself to be attracted to. A distraction is a pleasant diversion that can either come from yourself – something you're attracted to – or a welcome interruption from someone else. Whether it's an interruption or a distraction, either one can break your focus and take you away from what you were doing. Interruptions and distractions can though, be managed.

## THREE WAYS TO MANAGE INTERRUPTIONS AND DISTRACTIONS

1. **Anticipate and plan for interruptions and distractions.** If you know that you are likely to get interruptions from other people, plan for them. Leave gaps in your day for the time that interruptions will take up. Let others know when you'll be available to deal with their questions and queries.

2. **Identify what it is that you are easily distracted by.** Once you're aware of what those things are, you can think how to avoid, manage or minimize them. If it's your phone or emails, turn them off. If it's other people, go somewhere where they can't interrupt or distract you. If it's your environment, find somewhere with few things that are likely to distract you.

3. **Anticipate your needs before you do something that needs your focus.** Whether you'll need particular information or resources, get what you need in advance and you'll be less likely to need to stop what you're doing and lose focus.

# Accept that distractions and interruptions will happen

Be patient. If you can't avoid interruptions, then deal with each interruption one at a time. Give your full attention to each person and each query or problem. This way, you will less stressed and more able to deal calmly and fully with anyone who wants your attention. And then you can return to what you were doing.

It's one of the reasons why practising a breathing meditation is so helpful.

In a meditation, when your attention is interrupted or distracted by a thought, you acknowledge it then return your focus back to your breathing. You don't berate yourself for losing focus, you simply begin again.

And so you do the same when the focus of whatever it is that you're doing is broken by a distraction or an interruption. You accept it, acknowledge it, and begin again. Whatever the interruption or distraction, you know that you can begin again every time. There's no need to berate yourself for being distracted or get wound up because you've been interrupted. You simply begin again.

## Exercise: Develop your ability to remain focused and engaged

- Choose an activity that you've been putting off and that you find difficult to focus on. It could be completing an application form, deleting emails and files on your computer or editing photos on your phone. It could be decluttering your wardrobe, sorting out kitchen cupboards, or, if you have one, clearing out the loft, shed or garage.
- Decide how much time you'll spend on the task. Whether it's 20 minutes or an hour or two, commit yourself to that time. Tell yourself you will spend the full 20 minutes or one or two hours doing the task.
- Get prepared: get whatever you might need to carry out the task.
- Then get started.
- Anytime you lose focus – you get interrupted or distracted – accept it, acknowledge it, and begin again. Don't berate yourself for being distracted or berate the other person for interrupting you. Just return to the task at hand. Begin again.

# Affirmations

Choose one or more of the affirmations below to encourage you:

- One step at a time.
- I stay in the moment.
- Think only about what I'm doing now.
- I am here. Now.
- If I lose my focus, I can begin again every time.
- I lost focus. I can begin again.
- No matter the interruptions and distractions. I can always begin again.

# Key points

- During busy, stressful periods, when there's so much to do and think about, a mindful approach can help you calm down, focus and engage with what you need to do. By accepting the situation you free your mind to prioritize your tasks and make a step-by-step plan to get things done. You can then keep yourself in the present, focusing on one step at a time.

- Your focused steady pace can, however, be broken by interruptions and distractions. In meditation, when your attention is interrupted or distracted by a thought, you acknowledge it then return your focus back to your breathing. And so you do the same when the focus of whatever it is that you're doing is broken by a distraction or an interruption. You accept it, acknowledge it, and begin again.

- **Set yourself an intention:** Choose an activity that you've been putting off and that you find difficult to focus on. Decide how much time you'll spend on the task. Get prepared; get whatever you might need to carry out the task. Then get started. Anytime you lose focus – you get interrupted or distracted – accept it, acknowledge it, and begin again.

# Day 16

**AIM**
To do less and slow down.

**THOUGHT FOR TODAY**
*'There is more to life than increasing its speed.'*

*Gandhi*

# Zen tale: A gallop

A man was walking down the road when he saw a horse galloping towards him. It seemed that the rider was in a great hurry and had somewhere important to go.

'What's the rush? Where are you going?' asked the man.

'I don't know!' shouted the rider. 'Ask the horse!'

It's easy to let life run away with you like the horse was doing with the rider. So often, we rush through life doing so much that we don't engage with what is already here, now. Life is short. Doing too much, rushing from one thing to another, is not a good way to work or live.

You *can*, though, rein in your horse and slow down. Slowing down is a calmer and more peaceful way to approach your life.

Start by doing less.

## Exercise: Doing less

Are you doing too much? Filling your day with things to do could mean that you are constantly trying to get ahead of yourself. And that's not mindful! Instead, take a step back and see if there are activities, tasks and commitments – at work, with friends and family – you could let go of so that you can stop rushing and live life at a more relaxed, slower pace.

- **Start by identifying your commitments.** Write down daily, weekly and monthly tasks, activities, duties and commitments. Then add to your list, the hobbies, interests and social engagements you have.
- **Identify what to keep.** Decide which things you *have* to do. Then think about what you really *want* to do and what you enjoy doing. Highlight or put a tick next to each of those tasks and activities. These are your priorities.
- **Identify what to let go of.** Now look at what's left on your list. How do you feel about each activity? Put a line through

the things that you don't like, don't want or don't have the time to keep doing. Be honest with yourself. If you feel that you 'should' keep something on the list, know that for now, all you have to do is ask yourself, 'Do I like doing this? Do I want to keep doing it? Do I like doing it but I don't have room for it in my life right now?'

- **Read back over the list.** For each activity, task or duty you've crossed out, ask yourself, 'On a scale of 1–10, how much does it matter to me?' (10 being that you're not sure and 1 being that you definitely don't want to keep doing it.) Which commitments, tasks or activities have you rated with a number 5 or less? Which of those with a rating under 5 can you let go of; no longer do or be part of? What tasks can you give away; delegate and get someone else to do?

- **Let go of one thing.** You don't need to cut out everything at once – just letting go of one commitment for now is a good start. Once you've adjusted to that, let go of the next thing.

# Think positive!

Focus on what you have to gain from the moment you let go.

If you are struggling to let things go, realize that at the time, based on what you knew and how you felt then, your decision to do something – to commit yourself to something – *was* the right one.

Now, however, you realize it's not for you. Perhaps your circumstances have changed and you have new obligations. Maybe you've simply had a change of heart; you did enjoy what you were doing but now your feelings have changed, you realize that the situation isn't right for you. Accept that. Let go of the past and begin again in the present.

## Slowing down

As well as letting go of some of your commitments and activities, moving at a slower, more relaxed pace helps you better engage with what you are doing and what is happening in the present moment.

Writing in the *Telegraph* newspaper in November 2021, Helen McNutt described how, once her baby started sleeping through the night (and as a result, Helen was getting a good night's sleep) she started getting up early to write.

'It was winter. I was expecting to hate the cold, dark mornings, but I fell in love with them. It was the only time of day when things were quiet and still. I'd open the curtains a crack to look at the stars, glimpsing out every now and then as I wrote, watching the dawn creep softly though the trees. It was as if I was part of the morning, not just someone rushing through. Six years on, winter is still my favourite time.'

## Habit to develop

Like Helen, you could start your day a little slower. Try getting up 15 or 30 minutes earlier. Move calmly and slowly. Don't use the time to fit more in. Just choose to do something quiet and peaceful; meditate, write in your journal, read, listen to music or a podcast, practise yoga. Or simply be; simply sit and stare.

If you start your day slower you may also find that you can carry that calmer slower, pace with you throughout the rest of your day.

How much earlier could you easily get up? Make an intention today, that tomorrow you will get up a little bit earlier and spend the time doing something slow and calming.

## Spend time pottering

When you're pottering – whether it's in your home or garden – you're going contentedly from one simple easy-to-achieve task to the next. You're occupied, but not with anything especially demanding.

Sorting through the contents of drawers, rearranging cupboards, sorting things into piles, rearranging books and objects are all examples of pottering. So are watering plants, pruning and dead heading.

A key aspect of pottering is the slow pace at which you do it; you're unhurried, free of stress and responsibility. Whether it's half an hour, an hour or a whole morning, with unstructured downtime doing something that is slightly useful you are engaged in the gentlest of ways. The outcome of which is that your mind is rested and you are relaxed.

There's no pressure with pottering; you don't have to rush, nothing has to be completed; you can always pick it up where you left off and begin again another time.

## Slow food

How often do you gulp down some breakfast before racing out the door or wolf down a sandwich in your lunch break? Perhaps, at the end of the day, you're too tired to cook and you just stuff down a takeaway in front of the TV? When life is fast, eating quickly or on the go can become the norm. We shovel food into our mouths – sometimes spending the mealtime texting, scrolling through social media or working – without paying much attention to what we're eating.

But it doesn't have to be like this!

'Slow food' is about the experience of sourcing, preparing, and enjoying the process. The slow food movement (www.slowfood.org. uk) was founded as an antidote to the rise of fast food and fast life. Everything that mindless eating and fast food is, slow food isn't. It supports the awareness of good food, the enjoyment of eating and a slow pace of life. A life in which meals are not eaten on the run, with little regard for where your food comes from, how it's produced, prepared and consumed.

Slowing down to cook, eat and drink intentionally are part of developing a more healthy relationship with food. With the simple act of cooking and eating more slowly, everything slows down. Your meals become a mindful pleasure, not a thing to rush through, between other events in your day.

## Exercise: Practise eating more slowly and patiently

Mindful eating is a mindful activity you can easily include in your life. It's not difficult. You've got to eat. You just do it more slowly, mindfully. It takes five, ten or fifteen minutes extra each meal. You take smaller bites and chew each bite a little bit more slowly and for a tiny bit longer. Put your fork down every few mouthfuls.

Eating slowly, and paying attention to what you are eating, is mindful eating. You're more likely to notice flavours and textures and be more aware of when you are full. Be in the moment, rather than rushing through a meal thinking about what you need to do next. Put everything else to one side. When you eat, eat.

Each day, choose one meal that you will eat slowly and mindfully.

**FOUR SLOW HABITS TO DEVELOP**

1. **Give yourself more time.** If you're constantly rushing to appointments or other places you have to be, it's simply because you don't allot enough time. If you think it only takes you 30 minutes to get somewhere, perhaps give yourself 45 minutes so you can go at a leisurely pace and not get stressed if delays occur on the way.

2. **Do it in slow motion.** Slowing down takes practice. Whatever you're in the middle of doing, when you're aware that you're speeding up, slow it down by 25 percent. It might seem like a strange suggestion but try and imagine moving in slow motion. Whether it's typing on a keyboard, making a meal or a cup of tea, or cleaning the house, take your time and move slowly. Make your actions deliberate, not rushed and random.

3. **Write the word 'breathe' on a sticky note.** Place the note on a door, a mirror, your computer, or on the fridge, to remind you to slow down, breathe and bring yourself into the moment. Take a couple of minutes to stop and focus on breathing. Simply count to three on the in breath and count to five on each out breath.

4. **Practise yoga and Tai Chi.** Moving meditations such as yoga and Tai Chi integrate slow movements, physical postures, focused intentions, and breathing techniques. The slow gentle movements connect mind, body and soul so that they are in harmony with each other.

## Affirmations

- Do less.
- Slow. Down.
- My breath, and with it, my mind, are slowing down.
- Better to slow down than to break down.

# Key points

- So often, without realizing it, we find ourselves rushing through life doing too much and constantly trying to get ahead. And that's not mindful!

- Take a step back to identify activities, tasks and commitments you could let go of. You will be moving towards engaging with life more fully and more mindfully. Moving at a slower, more relaxed pace helps you better engage with what you are doing and what is happening in the present moment.

- **Set yourself an intention:** Today, choose one activity, duty or commitment that, from now on, you are going to let go of and stop doing. Once you've let go, remind yourself not to use the extra time to fit more in. You are aiming for a slower, more relaxed pace of life – a pace that allows you to better engage with what you are doing and what is happening in the present moment.

# Day 17

## AIM
To experience wonder and awe.

## THOUGHT FOR TODAY
*Awe and wonder: it's in everything. Everywhere. All The Time.*

Meditation, doing less, slowing down and focusing on one thing at a time as you attend to your daily activities and routines all helps train your mind to be in the present. And yet, it's still easy to get so caught up in everyday life that you miss out on opportunities to experience moments of awe and wonder.

There will though, have been times when you've been so moved by something – an amazing sunset for example, or a breathtaking view, or an uplifting piece of music – that you were stopped in your tracks; you were filled with wonder, admiration and awe.

Moments of awe – the combination of wonder, admiration and reverence – that we feel as a result of experiencing something beautiful, sublime, grand or powerful, are standout moments that set themselves over and above the ordinary aspects of our day.

## Awe-inspiring moments

When was the last time you had an awe-inspiring moment. Did anything on the list below move you; fill you with wonder and amazement?

- a view, a landscape or a cityscape
- the power of the ocean, a river or a waterfall
- a sunrise or a sunset
- a piece of music, a beautiful ballad, powerful rock or opera music, an organ recital, a symphony orchestra
- a firework display
- a star-filled sky

Although dramatic vistas such as canyons and mountains and the huge forces of a thunderstorm, tornado or volcano are awe inspiring, awe isn't just prompted by physical size. Any transcendent phenomenon or happening that goes beyond your ordinary experience of the world can induce feelings of awe and wonder.

Witnessing exceptional human or animal ability and skill, acts of courage, bravery, patience, kindness and compassion can inspire awe and wonder. So can being in the presence of another person's fame, prestige, power or authority.

Pregnancy and birth can create feelings of awe. And, although not easy, witnessing death can have an element of wonder too. The supernatural, spiritual and religious experiences, religious gatherings, ritual and prayer can be profound sources of awe. So can big ideas and complex concepts.

Being part of a collective act – dancing, singing in a choir or with a crowd, being part of a ceremony, concert or political march can literally move you.

The arts – visual art, sculpture, music, film, literature and poetry – can move you.

The phenomena of nature can inspire feelings of awe and wonder. It could be the delicacy and intricacy of a spider's web or the flowers growing through a crack in the pavement. A murmuration of starlings – the sight of thousands of birds swooping, twisting and turning overhead in perfect formation – is an incredible wildlife phenomenon to witness.

## Ephemeral but everlasting

Moments of awe and wonder stop us in our tracks and completely engage us with what's happening in front of us. We are immediately brought to the present; to the here and now.

Moments of awe and wonder soon pass. They are ephemeral – short-lived and transitory – but the experience may be so awesome that it remains with you a long time after. In a 2021 article for digital magazine psyche.co, Summer Allen describes her experience:

'On a crisp, clear day in January about four years ago, my children and I joined a few thousand Rhode Islanders in a protest march against a recent change in law that restricted the number of refugees who could enter the United States. As I held the hand of my four-year-old son, I was overcome with emotion. "No hate, no fear, refugees are welcome here," the crowd chanted as we marched through the streets ... With a tightness in my chest and tears in my eyes, I could barely join along without choking up. At the time, I didn't have a word to describe exactly what it was that I was feeling, but now I do: awe.'

Experiencing awe and wonder take you out of yourself. You're less focused on yourself, you feel more connected to the world and – as

Summer Allen discovered on the Rhode Island march – to other people. Your perspective shifts; you become aware that you are more than just yourself, you are a part of a greater whole and something larger than yourself.

## Wonder, awe and spirituality

*'Just as a candle cannot burn without fire, we cannot live without a spiritual life.'*

*Buddha*

The sense of connection to something – other people, nature, etc. – that fills you with wonder is the essence of spirituality. You might associate the word 'spirituality' with religion, the supernatural and the mystical. But spirituality is simply a sense of being connected to and being part of something bigger and more eternal than both the physical and yourself.

Certainly, for many religions, spirituality is an important aspect; however, you don't have to be religious in order to have a spiritual experience. Any experience that connects you to something in life larger than yourself – that inspires you with awe and wonder – can move your spirit and be a spiritual experience.

A spiritual experience, a moment of awe, can also help you to feel grounded in the present and yet connected to the past and the future. As the singer Guy Garvey, reflecting on the death of his father and the subsequent birth of his son, noted in a 2022 BBC radio interview, 'I realized life doesn't start and end with me. It started before me and it continues after me. It's not all about me.'

### Exercise: Spiritual connections

Think about what you already do that makes you feel connected. Perhaps it's gazing at the moon and the stars, being outdoors experiencing nature. Perhaps it's playing a team sport or cheering your team along with ten thousand other people. It might be singing in a choir or being at a music festival.

In your journal, write down what experiences and situations fill you with awe and wonder. Describe too, what for you is a spiritual experience; makes you feel connected to something bigger than yourself.

There's always room for more awe, wonder and connection. Over the next few pages are some more ideas and suggestions. Any time you experience something new, add it to your list.

## Experience more nature

Nature and the elements of the natural world – trees and plants, animals, hills and mountains, rivers and seas, and numerous other features of the earth – offer so much as a source of awe and wonder. Watching the wind blow through the trees, sensing the power of the sea, gazing at the enormity of a star-filled sky – these are the kind of moments when we can easily experience being part of something bigger, more eternal than both the physical and ourselves.

Nature connects the past, present and future. It can anchor you and give you perspective, enabling you to be aware of where you are and how you're connected in the greater scheme of things. And there's so much to be aware of! Step back to look at the big picture – the hills and valleys, the landscapes and the views, the rivers and seascapes. Look at the small details – a leaf, a flower, a blade of grass, a shell, a feather, an insect, a spider's web. See them in greater detail. Look for colours, patterns and symmetry.

Be aware too, that nature isn't just in the country, the parks and gardens. It's all around you in the streets and buildings in the towns and cities. Wherever you are, nature is always there.

### THE SCIENCE

In 2020, professor of psychology at University of California Dacher Keltner and his colleagues carried out a study which showed that regularly experiencing awe is a simple way to boost our emotional wellbeing.

In the study, participants took 15-minute 'awe walks' once a week for eight weeks. They were asked tap into their sense of curiosity and wonder, to consciously be aware of and appreciate the world around them. As a result, participants reported increased positive emotions and less distress in their daily lives.

One of the key features of awe is that it promotes a positive sense of perspective between yourself and the bigger picture and power of the world around you. There's a sense of feeling small in the grand scheme of things. But isn't feeling small a negative thing? Yes, but with awe experiences, it's your problems that shrink rather than your sense of self-worth.

## A walk on the wild side

Awe is something that Jake Tyler regularly experienced between 2016 and 2018 on his walk around the coast of England, Wales and Scotland. In the two years before his epic walk, 30-year-old Jake was overweight, had a drinking problem and felt broken. Jake was suicidal.

He quit his job in London and moved back to the town he grew up in, to stay with his mum. After a few weeks of doing very little except eat junk food and watch TV, things began to change for Jake when he decided to go for daily walks with his Mum's dog, Reggie.

Jake says that the walks helped him understand that 'the world is pretty amazing and nature is lovely'. Realizing how healing being outside had been for him, Jake was inspired to do an epic 3000-mile walk circumnavigating Britain. Describing his experience in his book *A Walk From The Wild Edge* Jake writes that, 'Everything felt completely stripped back. I was on my own in this natural setting and I felt reset. I realized everything had been here before and would be here long after me. I felt insignificant but in a good way, a way that made me wonder at it all rather than making me feel small.'

### DID YOU KNOW?

Varieties Corpus (www.varietiescorpus.com) is a website where you can share and learn about self-transcendent and awe-inspiring experiences.

## Exercise: Get more Wow! in your life

As well as the wonders of nature, there are many other opportunities to experience awe and wonder. You just need to be aware of what they are and engage with them. Here are some suggestions for you to explore.

- **Watch natural history programmes on TV.** These programmes can give you a sense of wonder and appreciation for the world you live in. So can NASA's 'Astronomy Picture of the Day': apod.nasa.gov/apod/astropix.html
- **Zoom in.** With a simple magnifying glass you can change the perspective of the most simple ordinary things. Find something to look at with a magnifying glass – a leaf, a flower or an insect. Or take a photo and then zoom in for a closer look.
- **Stop and stare.** Whenever you enter grand lobbies and atriums, churches and cathedrals, mosques and temples, stop and stare. Look up and look all around you.
- **Consider a big idea.** Wonder and speculate as to how and why. Think, for example, about clouds, waves, or rainbows. What's happening there? You can also contemplate the wonders of science and technology.
- **Airplanes, MRI and ultrasound scans, TVs and radios.** How do they work? What about indoor plumbing? How do you think that works? Think about it, then Google it to find out and be further amazed.
- **Watch the earth rise.** The sun stays in its position at the centre of our solar system. It doesn't rise and set. But it appears to rise and set because of the Earth's rotation on its axis. Knowing this, one evening, go outside somewhere that you can watch the sunset. Conceive the notion not of the sun setting but the Earth rising and be aware that you live on a planet spinning in space.
- **Listen to music.** Make music. Listening to or playing any form of music has the potential to elicit awe – beautiful songs, powerful lyrics, strong rhythms and beats and full volume – so many aspects of music have the power to move us. Making music with others – be it in a choir, band or orchestra – increases the likelihood of awe because of the synchronicity.

- **Move in unison with others.** Humans have a natural proclivity for synchronized movement. Moving together can move you emotionally. Take part in shared movement such as dance, exercise, or even walking with one or more friends.
- **Take in visual art or film.** Visits to art galleries and museums – in person or online – public art and sculpture, and films with stunning visual elements, watched on the big screen can all provoke awe.
- **Watch slow motion.** Ordinary events can become extraordinary occurrences when presented in a unique way. Look, for example, at the Slo Mo Guys slow-motion video of drops of coloured water falling into a bowl of milk on YouTube.
- **Witness someone doing something amazing.** Be inspired; read or watch films and documentaries about other people's skills and talents or bravery and courage.
- **Spend time with someone who is spiritual.** Who do you already know who has balance and a sense of perspective; who has a calm concern and rapport with other people? It could be someone with a sense of wonder, someone who seeks out beauty and peace in the things they do. Spend time with spiritual people you admire. Their attitude will inspire you.

# Affirmations

- Pause for moments of awe. Wonder at the beauty of life.
- Awe and wonder. It's in everything. Everywhere. All The Time.

# Key points

- Moments of awe – the combination of wonder, admiration and reverence – that we feel as a result of experiencing something beautiful, sublime, grand or powerful, are standout moments that set themselves over and above the ordinary aspects of our day. They stop us in our tracks and completely engage us. We are immediately brought to the present; to the here and now.

- Experiencing awe and wonder takes you out of yourself. You're less focused on yourself, you feel more connected to the world and to other people. Your perspective shifts. You become aware that you are more than just yourself – you are a part of a greater whole and something larger than yourself.

- **Set yourself an intention:** Make yourself aware of the people, places, experiences and situations that already fill you with awe and wonder. Then, develop that new awareness: commit to experiencing moments of awe and wonder more often.

# Day 18

## AIM

To include more small pleasures in your life.

## THOUGHT FOR TODAY:

*What is this life if, full of care,*
*We have no time to stand and stare.*
*No time to stand beneath the boughs*
*And stare as long as sheep or cows.*

*W. H. Davies*

The first four lines of W.H Davies's poem remind us that too often, we are so caught up in cares and worries and rushing from one thing to the next, that we have no time to stand and stare. It's not just the moments of awe and wonder that we miss, we miss the small pleasures that can fully engage us in the present and give us moments of joy.

The small pleasures are of course, the smallest of things. You just need to be more aware of them, engage with them and appreciate them.

What, for you, makes for small pleasures? Maybe eating the froth on the cappuccino is a small pleasure? Or eating a perfectly ripe pear or peach? Do you enjoy foraging for wild blackberries in the autumn? Perhaps one of your small pleasures is the old comfortable clothes that you put on when you want to relax? What about a bubble bath or a hot shower? Warm towels? Maybe, on a cold morning, it's putting on an item of clothing that's been sitting on a hot radiator?

Perhaps it's sitting in front of an open fire, or sitting in the sun, or taking a walk in the rain? Is kitchen dancing one of your favourite things? What about car dancing? Singing in the shower?

Maybe fresh clean sheets are a small pleasure for you? A lie in? An afternoon nap? Reading a book by one of your favourite authors? Scrolling through photos of happy times in your life? A kiss, a cuddle or holding hands? Or a foot massage? Maybe talking to your dog or cat is one of your small pleasures?

And, as odd as it may seem to other people, maybe one of your small pleasures is time spent ironing tea towels and pillowcases?

Writer and author Neil Pasricha has managed to identify 1000 small pleasures. He's listed them on his website 1000AwesomeThings. com. Here's a few that might resonate with you:

- spotting dogs who look like their owners
- popping bubble wrap
- when the bass kicks in
- drying off in the sun after swimming
- writing with a really good pen

- turning over your pillow
- slurping hot soup on a cold night
- somehow finishing your shampoo and conditioner bottles at the same time.

When you make an effort to be aware of the small pleasures in life and take notice of what's happening around you that pleases you, you'll be surprised at just how many things give moments of joy. And, with each small pleasure, you are completely engaged and in the moment.

## Exercise: A list of small pleasures

There's a world of small pleasures which can bring you moments of joy every day.

Raise your awareness. In your journal, make a list of small pleasures and favourite things, the ordinary and the extraordinary, the familiar and the new, the little things and the tiny things, the cheap and the expensive.

Add to your list every time you think of something else that brings a small pleasure. And whether they are old or new pleasures, resolve to indulge in them more often. Over the next couple of pages are some suggestions for adding more small pleasures to your life.

## The pleasures of beauty

'Breathe in beauty, breathe out Joy.'

*Eliza Dodd*

Beauty can be found in sounds, shapes and colours, designs and patterns. Beauty is, of course, in the eye of the beholder. What do you perceive to be beautiful? What sights and sounds, tastes and smells please you? Consciously look for and appreciate instances of beauty;

art and architecture for example, people, animals, music, wildlife and nature all have the potential for beauty. Beauty is uplifting and inspiring; being aware of and appreciating beauty can give you a sense of calm and peace.

## Habit to develop

Although you can admire and enjoy beauty without feeling a need to do anything about it, you could start a collection of photos of things you find beautiful – anything from a view and a sunset to the details of or a flower, a shell or a feather – to gaze at whenever you need a small pleasure.

## The pleasure of pottering

On Day 16 you read about the importance of slowing down – that moving at a slower, more relaxed pace allows you to better engage with what you're doing and what's happening in the present moment.

Specific slow activities are also small pleasures. 'Slow food' – the awareness of good food, the enjoyment of eating and a slow pace of life – can be a small pleasure. As can the activity of pottering. When you're pottering – whether it's in your home or garden – you're going contentedly from one simple easy-to-achieve task to the next. The unhurried, relaxed approach that makes pottering a mindful activity also contributes to it being a small pleasure; you are engaged in the gentlest of ways. The outcome of which is that your mind is rested and you are relaxed. There's no pressure with pottering; nothing has to be completed, you can always pick it up where you left off and begin again another time.

## The pleasure of music

Listening to or playing music, singing and dancing to music is a source of numerous small pleasures; the pleasure of music can range from being totally energizing, to calming and relaxing. Make a playlist of music songs that give you pleasure. Sing out loud and dance like no one's watching.

## The small pleasures in nature

Whenever you can, try and spend some time of your day or your week in nature. Most of us have somewhere near to the natural world, even if it's only a small park or garden. With more than 62,000 urban green spaces in Great Britain, one should never be too far away. The Wildlife Trusts (www.wildlifetrusts.org) have a searchable online map of its nature reserves, almost all of which have free entry; it also provides a list of accessible nature reserves. And Ordnance Survey's Greenspace (getoutside.ordnancesurvey.co.uk/greenspaces/) shows thousands of green spaces for leisure and recreation.

## Small birds; small pleasures

Looking out of a window and watching the birds is another small pleasure. You don't need any special equipment, but you could try hanging a bird feeder outside a window or, if there's space, fit a small wooden nesting box to a tree or under a windowsill. See the RSPB website (rspb.org.uk) for more information on feeding, sheltering and watching birds.

## Beginner's mind and small pleasures

On Day 12 and Day 13 you read how a beginner's mind can raise your awareness and help you appreciate people, places, experiences and events as if for the first time. Reminding yourself of the benefits and enjoyment your possessions give you is another way to access small pleasures.

## Gratitude

*'Hem your blessings with thankfulness so they don't unravel.'*

*Author unknown*

Gratitude, like mindfulness, is a way of noticing and relating to life. Gratitude typifies mindfulness; it involves being aware and acknowledging the positive things – the small pleasures – in your life right now.

Writing in the *Guardian* newspaper in November 2020, journalist Kathryn Bromwich described how, for the past six years she'd been writing down three good things that happened in her day, every day. 'It doesn't matter how big or small they are. It could be having pastries in bed. Spotting a fox in the garden. Successfully descaling a kettle ... I have found it vital ... to focus on the things that have gone right. Left unattended, my thoughts have a tendency to slip into a downward spiral.'

The smallest things can make the biggest difference. Much of life is made up of small things and moments, one thing following another. Gratitude happens best when you notice the small pleasures around you; the things that often go unnoticed or unappreciated.

## Exercise: Make it a habit

- At the end of each day, identify and reflect on three positive things that happened in your day – the small pleasures that you sought out or that happened without you planning them. Actively look for things to appreciate. Appreciate just knowing that you had good in your day so that whatever else happened, whatever difficulties you experienced, you know that there was some positivity there.
- You might want to write down the three positive things in a notebook or journal, or you might simply reflect on what those things are as you are getting ready for bed. Even if you get to the end of the day feeling that not much went right, instead of dwelling on what went wrong, reflect on the small pleasures – what was good and nice – and you'll know that it wasn't all bad.
- Just make an effort for a couple of weeks to identify the good things – the small joys – in your day. After a while, identifying and reflecting on the small pleasures will become a habit. A mindful habit.

## Try it now

Think of three small positive events that happened yesterday. Then at the end of today, reflect on three good things that happened today.

## THE SCIENCE

A study by associate professor Nicole Mead and her colleagues found that including simple pleasures in your day can not only help offset daily irritations and minor annoyances that might occur, but those same simple pleasures can also support you in achieving what you set out to do that day.

Published in 2016 by the University of Chicago *Journal of the Association for Consumer Research*, Professor Mead and her colleagues discovered that on days when participants in the study experienced little in the way of small pleasures, minor difficulties and problems hindered progress on the tasks and activities they had planned to do.

In contrast, when participants recorded several small pleasures in their day, small annoyances had no negative impact. Rather, the participants stuck to their goals and made steady progress with the tasks they had set out for themselves that day.

'Our results suggest that the real power of simple pleasures that make us feel good seems to come from when things aren't going well. A simple pleasure seems to restore people's psychological reserves to do well,' says Professor Mead.

Typically, for most of us when our day isn't going quite as we hoped, when interruptions and small annoyances are presenting us with difficulties, we put aside small pleasures. But according to Professor Mead's research, depriving yourself of small pleasures, will hinder, not help you make progress with what you are hoping to achieve.

So, when little irritations and minor annoyances are getting to you, take a break and indulge in a small pleasure before resuming whatever it was you were working on.

# Affirmations

- I will make time for small pleasures.
- Slow down and enjoy the small pleasures.
- I recognize the power of small pleasures.
- Life is full of small wonders and moments of joy. Look for them!
- The littlest things can hold the greatest meaning.

# Key points

- Small pleasures can fully engage us in the present and give us moments of joy.

- The small pleasures in life are the smallest of things. You just need to be more aware of them, engage with them and appreciate them.

- Actively look for things to appreciate. At the end of each day, identify and reflect on three positive things that happened in your day; the small pleasures that either you sought out or that happened without you planning them.

- **Set yourself an intention:** Make a list of small pleasures and favourite things. Add to your list every time you think of something else that brings a small pleasure.

# Day 19

**AIM**

To experience a state of flow and just being.

**THOUGHT FOR TODAY**

*'How can I be still? By flowing with the stream.'*

*Lao Tzu*

Today's thought – a quote by ancient Chinese philosopher Lao Tzu – suggests that the way to be still – to be calm and peaceful – is 'by flowing with the stream'. What does that mean? How can you be still by 'flowing with the stream?'

It may seem like a contradiction in terms, but actually, it expresses a truth. Research carried about during the 1980s and 1990s, Professor Mihaly Csikszentmihalyi – a psychology professor at the University of Chicago – can help to explain this paradoxical suggestion.

Professor Csikszentmihalyi began researching the concept of 'flow' as a result of observing artists who appeared to lose themselves in their work. In interviews with Professor Csikszentmihalyi, many of the artists explained that when they were completely engaged with what they were doing, it felt like a water current was carrying them along; that they were 'flowing with the stream'. Professor Csikszentmihalyi named this concept the state of 'flow.'

It's not, however, just artists that experience 'flowing with the stream' and being in a state of 'flow'. You have, too. Whenever you've been doing something that so absorbed you and time passed without you realizing it, you have experienced being in a state of flow. As you engaged with what you were doing, your awareness merged with whatever activity it was that you were doing. Everything – time, the activity, your energy and focus – flowed effortlessly along. You were living from moment to moment.

A state of flow is a mindful state. Your mind is so focused and engaged, it doesn't wander off, nothing can distract you. No thoughts or concerns about the past or future enter into your head. The level of engagement absorbs you so deeply and holds your attention. Your thoughts are positive and in tune with what you're doing. You're in a state of flow; it's as if a water current is carrying you along.

## Exercise: Discover your mindful flow experiences

- What do you like doing? What activities can you immerse yourself in for an hour or more? In your journal, write down the things you enjoy doing; hobbies, sports, activities and interests. They are activities during which you experience flow – they keep you so absorbed that you are constantly in the here and now.

- Add to your list anything you used to do that, although you no longer do it, you remember it as being something that you enjoyed and it kept you fully engaged and absorbed. Consider trying those activities again.
- Know that when you need to bring together your mind, body and environment for a period of time that keeps you present, they are activities where you can easily experience flow.

## The state of flow

When you are in the state of flow:

- You know what you are doing and what the next step will be. There's no uncertainty or doubt.
- There's a balance between challenge and skills. For example, when you do a jigsaw puzzle, if it's too difficult you may give up; if it's too easy you may become bored or do it mindlessly.
- You let go of your sense of self and any worries, concerns or problems.
- You feel at one with what you are doing.
- You're content, although you don't really notice it at the time because you're so absorbed in what you're doing.
- You're doing it for the experience, not for any sort of result. It's intrinsically rewarding
- Time passes without you noticing.
- You're completely focused and engaged.

## Being in flow

When you are in a state of flow you are just 'being' – you are at one with the effortless unfolding of time and the activity you are involved in.

In meditation, you practise being aware of and disengaging from what your mind is doing and, instead, you just let it be. You let your mind exist in a state of simply being. Each time your mind wanders into 'doing' – thinking, worrying, remembering planning, berating etc. – you return your awareness to your breathing – to simply being.

A state of flow is a state of being. When you are in a state of flow, rather than doing, your mind and body are being. It's the same when you experience moments of awe, wonder and small pleasures – you are just being.

With a flow activity, although you are doing something, your focus isn't on achieving something. Yes, you might complete the puzzle or finish the book, but that's not your main aim; you're not aiming to get something done. If something does get completed or finished, that's a bonus. But in being, there's no standard to be reached, nothing to judge or compare it with, nothing to finish, nowhere to get to; you are simply being part of a moment-by-moment experience, being present and engaged with whatever is here, right now.

Being mode is not, however, a state in which all activity has to stop. Doing and being are both states of mind that can define any activity or level of activity. If, for example, you are washing up with the aim of getting it done – doing it 'properly', getting it over and done with and out of the way – then you would be in doing mode. And that's ok; most of the time, things do need to get done. But if you approach the washing up in being mode, then the activity is accepted and engaged with for its own sake in its own time.

## Exercise: Getting more flow in your life

Here are some ideas of how to be in flow more often in your life:

- **Play a sport.** Badminton, squash, table tennis, rugby, football, bowling or billiards – whatever it is, everything in sport happens in the moment.

- **Flow activities.** Yoga, boxing, judo, darts, archery, rock climbing, canoeing and swimming – these are just a few examples of flow activities. Focusing on each individual movement forces your mind to live in that single moment with your body.
- **Play a team sport.** Tennis or football, whatever it is, everything in sport happens in the moment. No time to worry about the last shot because another one is coming right back at you!
- **Join a dance class.** Ballet, ballroom, hip hop, tap – or just sing and dance along to your favourite tunes in the kitchen. You'll become immersed in the music and really be in the moment.
- **Take up a creative interest.** Gardening, cooking, painting, drawing, calligraphy, colouring in, crochet, woodcarving, model building, juggling – whatever it is, for many people, a creative activity is a place to dwell happily in the present moment.
- **Play or learn to play a musical instrument.** Piano, guitar, drums, flute or harmonica – whatever it is, for many people, playing an instrument is a mindful meditation in itself.
- **Play games and do puzzles.** Card and board games, computer games, jigsaws, crosswords, sudoku, Wordle – all require a level of concentration and provide a challenge that will have you totally absorbed.
- **Read a book or watch a film.** It could be a gripping thriller, science fiction or a clever comedy – whatever the genre, a good book or film can capture your attention completely.

## Writing 'Morning Pages'

Morning Pages are three pages of longhand writing written first thing each morning. The concept of Morning Pages comes from the book *The Artist's Way* by Julia Cameron. She originally designed the Morning Pages to help artists break through their creative blocks. However, this approach to journaling is valuable for anyone; it can empty your mind and help you to gain clarity, focus, and direction.

You are encouraged to write about anything and everything that comes into your mind – a stream of consciousness, a state of being and the experience of flow.

---

### Exercise: Writing Morning Pages

- Get yourself a notebook and a pen that is easy to write with.

- Get up a little bit earlier every morning and complete three pages of longhand stream-of-consciousness writing. It doesn't matter what you write. There is no right or wrong way to fill your pages. You could write down what dreams you had the night before, concerns and worries you have, what the cat did yesterday, the chores you need to do, what your tea or coffee tastes like, a shopping list, a to-do list, affirmations and so on. You could write down ideas, things you've enjoyed and not enjoyed recently or in the past, what's annoying you, what you resent, any regrets you might have or what you're looking forward to. You simply write whatever comes into your head. You let the words flow.

- Julia Cameron recommends that what you write is just for you at the time you are writing it; that you don't share it with others or even re-read any of the pages at a later date. This makes it more likely that you will be able to write what's on your mind – no matter how petty, trivial, mad or bad – write without fear of judgment. Just write three pages of anything. And then do three more pages tomorrow. Begin again.

---

# Affirmations

- I am here. Now.
- I am.
- Just be.
- Let it be.
- Nothing to do. Nowhere to go.
- I am at one with the unfolding of time.

# Key points

- A state of flow is a mindful state. Your mind is so focused and engaged, it doesn't wander off. Nothing can distract you. No thoughts or concerns about the past or future enter into your head. The level of engagement absorbs you so deeply and holds your attention. Your thoughts are positive and in tune with what you're doing. You're in a state of flow, as if a water current is carrying you along.

- When you are in a state of flow you are just 'being'. You are at one with the effortless unfolding of time and the activity you are involved in. In being, there's no standard to be reached, nothing to judge or compare it with, nothing to finish, nowhere to get to. You are simply part of a moment-by-moment experience, being present and engaged with whatever is here, right now.

- **Set yourself an intention:** Today, choose to do one activity that you enjoy, that will keep you focused and engaged for half an hour or more.

# Day 20

## AIM

To have patience in the unfolding of events.

## THOUGHT FOR TODAY

*Patience is a state of grace; understanding and accepting that sometimes things must unfold in their own time.*

Patience can be challenging to develop and maintain in a world where everything is available and we are encouraged to get it, have it or be it right now.

Often, in a variety of situations, we may not even be aware that we're being impatient because our mind has already jumped ahead to how and where we want things to be. When we realize that something or someone is going to take longer than we'd like, we start looking for ways to hurry things up. We try to get somewhere more quickly, rush an outcome, or make the unknown known.

## Exercise: Patience

There are situations that try even the most patient among us. In your journal, note down which of these situations you have experienced recently.

- travel delays and traffic jams
- queues at the supermarket, bank or post office
- being unable to find something; phone, keys etc.
- being kept on hold on the phone or being transferred many times before being able to talk to the person that can help you
- a colleague taking too long to give you some information you need
- your child refusing to cooperate – again
- your partner forgetting to do something you asked them to do – again

Whatever the situation, in your journal, describe how you reacted. Were you stressed and agitated waiting for it to happen? Did you fuel your impatience with judgements about how wrong it all was or how long it was taking or how incompetent other people were?

As well as daily frustrations, what about long-term events? Whether it's a profession that takes many years to qualify in, finding somewhere new to live – to buy or rent – or recovering from an illness, situations like these can also test your patience. In your journal, note down a situation where you had to wait a long time for something to come into being.

# Patience: a state of grace

Even when you are aware that you are being impatient, you might think that the cause of your impatience is a specific event or the actions of other people. Actually, the cause is in your own mind – it's your reaction that causes impatience, not what is or isn't happening.

Just as mindful acceptance recognizes that something is what it is, so does patience. Mindful patience has the ability and willingness to let something be; to wait calmly without needing to change it to when you want it to be.

Patience is often seen as a virtue. It is an aspect of moral excellence – an ability to tolerate and endure under sufferance, to suppress restlessness or annoyance when confronted with delay. But in mindfulness, patience is not understood as a state of endurance and reluctant self-control. Instead, mindfulness understands patience as a state of grace; a state of effortless calm and goodwill; an ability to experience provocation, difficulties and delays, quietly and steadily with fortitude and calm.

## Exercise: Being aware of impatience

- Your ability to be patient, calm and accepting is so much easier when you are grounded in a daily experience of just being. Meditation gives you a break from doing. Meditation is just being. In meditation when you are aware of a thought, you acknowledge it, accept it and you let it pass. You are patient.
- You can do the same in everyday life.
- Start by being aware of the events, people and situations that trigger impatience for you. Write them down in your journal.
- Next, write down what might be a typical way that you would react. What do you say to yourself? What, if anything, do you do? Write about your reactions in your journal.

## Reframe the situation

On Day 11 you learned that when you give meaning to events and experiences – judge them, begrudge and resent them – not only do your thoughts about those events and experiences create difficulty and discomfort, but those thoughts get in the way of recognizing that whatever the situation, it will pass.

Even though you might not be able to control how and when things happen, you can control how you respond to a delay.

From now on, try to recognize when you're becoming impatient. Notice if your mind is agitated – are you feeling irritated, frustrated or annoyed? Is your body tense? Are you fuelling your impatience with judgements about how wrong it all is or how slow things are?

When there are delays and hold-ups, try not to judge. Instead, just as you would in an 'open monitoring' meditation, step back, observe and simply describe the situation. Recognize, for instance, 'I'm stuck in traffic' or, 'My child/elderly parent needs more time to do this.'

It is what it is. It only becomes something that frustrates you if you attribute a negative meaning to it.

When you are aware that you are becoming agitated, tell yourself: 'This too will pass.' Like clouds passing in the sky or leaves floating down a stream, things do move on. Remind yourself of this when you are waiting. However long the delay or the wait, it's not permanent. Time always passes, and how you feel during that time is of your own making. Change how you think about a delay and you will have a calmer, clearer mind.

## Get things into perspective

Getting a sense of perspective can help you be more patient. Gaining perspective means having a sense of where you are in the greater scheme of things, taking everything else into account and understanding the relative importance of things.

So often, it's the daily hassles that we get impatient about. But whatever it was that irked you, when you look back now – a day, a week or months later – it seems a lot less annoying; even rather trivial.

Perspective helps you to understand that, as frustrating as things might be at this moment, the situation will change. Life will continue and one way or another, things will work out. You might want for things to be different in the future, but in the present moment you accept things as they are and for what they are, knowing that this too will pass.

## DID YOU KNOW?

Certainly, there are situations in life where patience is not a virtue. Waiting to see if a health concern turns into something more serious before going to your doctor, for example is not patience; it's denial. So is staying in a situation that one way or another, is not safe for you and other people.

### Exercise: Practise patience

Practise being comfortable with sitting, doing nothing. If, when you have to wait, you become impatient or uncomfortable, instead of reading or getting your phone out or huffing and puffing, try just sitting there, looking around, taking in your surroundings. In a queue, just wait in line and watch and listen to what is going on around you.

You can even practise patience by making yourself wait. Next time, rather than choosing the shortest queue, choose the longest queue. Stand in line and just observe and listen to people around you.

## Be patient with other people

People might be physically slower, or slower to learn or understand, or slower at expressing themselves – describing or explaining something. Too often in these situations, when we realize that someone is going to take longer than we'd like, we start looking for ways to hurry things up.

But we each do things at a different pace. Having patience means accepting that people and situations develop at their own speed. Maybe it's the story you've heard someone tell many times before. But you don't tell them that. They enjoy reminiscing. Perhaps it's the supermarket checkout assistant chatting with a customer who has more than two or three people waiting behind them; patience and acceptance helps you to see the importance of these small exchanges between people.

You *can* choose to be accepting, patient and kind.

Impatience rarely gets others to move faster. In fact, it can interfere with their ability to think clearly and act competently. All you're doing is creating stress for them. Remind yourself that you're not helping anyone if you interact with them from a position of impatience and judgement.

Keep your mind and heart open. The world has got plenty of impatient, judgemental, unreasonable people in it, so try and be one of the patient ones.

## The power of patience

Writing in *Harvard Magazine* in 2013, professor of history of art and architecture Jennifer L. Roberts explains her belief in the importance of creating opportunities for her students to engage in what she describes as 'deceleration, patience, and immersive attention'.

All of her students have to write an intensive research paper based on a single work of art of their own choosing. In preparation for this, they are expected to go to Boston's Museum of Fine Arts, to look at the painting 'Boy with a Squirrel', by John Singleton Copley. Students are told to spend three full hours looking at the painting, (which Professor Roberts herself has done) noting down their evolving observations as well as the questions and speculations that arise from those observations.

Professor Roberts says that 'The time span is explicitly designed to seem excessive. Also crucial to the exercise is the museum or archive setting, which removes the student from his or her everyday surroundings and distractions.'

She writes that her students are resistant: 'How can there possibly be three hours' worth of incident and information on this small surface? How can there possibly be three hours' worth of things to see and think about in a single work of art? But after doing the assignment, students repeatedly tell me that they have been astonished by the potentials this process unlocked.'

Professor Roberts goes on to explain that 'It is commonly assumed that vision is immediate ... But what students learn in a visceral way in this assignment is that in any work of art there are details and orders and relationships that take time to perceive.'

In other words, just because you can see something or access it in some way doesn't mean that you can understand it. What turns seeing into understanding is time and patience.

Professor Robert's directive illustrates the idea that time is not a negative space to be tolerated or to be overcome. It is a formative force in itself.

## Wu wei: A time for everything

With patience, there is understanding and trusting that things develop in their own time; that life is a process of unfolding. With patience, you know that there's a time for everything and everything takes time.

On Day 16 you were encouraged to slow down; to recognize that being too busy – trying to fit too much into your day – can lead to impatience. Instead of rushing through life doing too much and constantly trying to get ahead of yourself, you were encouraged to set and maintain a slower pace of life.

On Day 19 you were introduced to the concept of being; to know that being gives you a break from doing. In being, there's nothing to do, nowhere to get to and nothing to finish; you are simply being part of a moment-by-moment experience, being present and engaged with whatever is here, right now.

Slowing down and just being reflects the Taoist concept of *wu wei*.

In Taoism – a tradition of philosophy and religious belief from ancient China – *wu wei* means living with the true nature of the world without obstructing the Tao (Tao being the natural order of the universe).

*Wu wei* is a state of being in which our actions and inaction are effortlessly in alignment with the ebb and flow of the natural world. There's no need to try to make things happen; instead, we just go with the flow, patiently letting things be and trusting that things will take their natural course in the same way that a river flowing through the landscape finds its natural course.

Taoism encourages us to live a life of balance and harmony; we can still be proactive but our actions fit into the natural pattern of the world.

Like mindfulness, Taoism encourages us to live with patience and trust. It suggests that we be comfortable doing less; that we conserve our physical, mental and emotional energy, knowing that things will eventually come into being.

*Wu wei* shows that when we do less, when we wait and watch, we see outside forces more clearly and make wiser moves.

## Try it now

The *Tao Te Ching* suggests we develop our understanding of the concept of non-action by observing the natural world. One way to do this is to plant some bulbs – daffodils and tulips – in the autumn. They will sit in the ground all winter, but then in their own time, in spring, they will appear out of the earth and come into flower. A reminder that there's a time for everything and everything in its time.

## Affirmations

Affirmations help keep your focus on what you want to become. Today, the aim is to develop patience in the unfolding of events:

- Today I choose patience.
- Time always passes. How I feel during that time is of my own making.
- I am willing to wait calmly without needing to change it to when I want it to be.

- Patience is easier when I stay in the present.
- I breathe in patience and breathe out calm.
- I trust that things develop in their own time; that life is a process of unfolding.
- There's a time for everything and everything takes time.
- Everything is happening when it should.
- All is for the best in this best of all possible worlds.
- When nothing is done, nothing is left undone.
- Everything will happen in its own time.
- I am exactly where I need to be right now.

# Key points

- Mindfulness understands patience not as a state of endurance and reluctant self-control, but as a state of grace; a state of effortless calm and goodwill, an ability to experience difficulties and delays quietly and steadily with fortitude and calm.

- However long a delay or the wait, it's not permanent. Time always passes, and how you feel during that time is of your own making. Change how you think about a delay and you will have a calmer, clearer mind.

- **Set yourself an intention:** Practise being patient. Starting today, do one activity every day for a week that requires patience. It could be a large jigsaw puzzle, sewing, knitting or embroidery, mending or constructing something. Whatever you choose, notice that little by little it comes into being; it comes about and is completed.

# Day 21

## INTENTION
To have a 'daily-ish' mindfulness practice.

## THOUGHT FOR TODAY
*'Habit is a cable; we weave a thread of it each day, and at last we cannot break it.'*

*Horace Mann*

Being more aware, acknowledging, accepting, being non-judgemental, letting go, beginning again, having patience and trust. These are all aspects of mindfulness that you've learned and been encouraged to practise in the last 20 days. You've been introduced to new ideas and concepts, new ways of thinking and doing. But how, you might ask, do you maintain these new ways of thinking and behaving so that they become second nature instead of being quite an effort?

Establishing and maintaining new ways of thinking and behaving are more likely to happen if you can accept them as being part of a process; a continual series of gradual changes that will take time to establish.

How long will that process take? Another three weeks? Three months or longer? It's different for everyone; there's no hard and fast rules, but the process is the same for any new way of thinking or doing, whether it's learning to play tennis or learning a language for example, or being mindful; it requires regular practice.

Of course, whatever it is you are learning to do differently, you have to be able to understand the ideas, principles and concepts. The exercises you are asked to do need to be interesting and challenging enough (but not too hard). But if you do understand the ideas and concepts and find the exercises interesting and challenging, then you are more likely to continue to practise the different aspects of mindfulness.

If you can see the benefits and feel that you are making progress that also makes it more likely that you will continue to practise mindfulness and it will eventually become second nature – your usual way of being and doing.

It's the regular practice that is key. As you will have read on Day 3, when you think or do things for the first time, you create new connections – 'neural pathways' – in your brain. Then, every time you repeat those thoughts or actions, every time you continue using these new pathways, they become stronger and more established.

It's like walking through a field of long grass, each step helps to create a new path and every time you walk that new path you establish a clear route which becomes easier to use the next time. It becomes a habit to use that route.

But you don't have to figure it all out at once!

You may remember reading what Dan Harris said on Day 1:

'I'd rather see people do five to ten minutes a day, but I'm quite familiar with the diabolical difficulty of habit formation. So I like to use two little slogans: "one minute counts" and "daily-ish." If you can set a loose goal and have a sense of experimentation and humour ... as you establish a habit, I think it's possible.'

Although Dan was referring to establishing meditation as a habit, the same approach is true for any aspect of mindfulness – awareness, non-judgement, or beginner's mind, for example – even short amounts of time on a "daily-ish" basis will help you establish a mindfulness practice as a habit.

## Managing slip-ups and setbacks

*'Drop by drop is the water pot filled.'*

Buddha

However, until those memory pathways are well established, it's entirely possible that you will slip back into old ways of thinking and behaving, being and doing. It's normal and it's to be expected. Understanding this – that setbacks are normal and to be expected – can help prevent you from feeling discouraged and giving up.

On Day 4, you learned that in meditation, each time you are aware that you have lost your focus – that your mind has wandered – rather than get frustrated and give up, you accept you've lost focus and simply return your attention back to your breathing. You begin again. The same approach applies to any aspect of mindfulness – if you lose focus, forget or neglect to practise an aspect of mindfulness for any length of time or in a particular situation, there's no need to berate yourself, feel discouraged and give up. Instead, you simply begin again.

Every day, one way or another, you get the chance to be mindful. Every day there are opportunities to be mindful.

Acceptance, non-judgement and beginner's mind are all inherent in establishing a mindfulness practice. Patience and trust are also part of the process of establishing and maintaining mindfulness in your life. Be patient and kind to yourself; don't think of relapses as failure, instead, think of relapses as part of the process of change; opportunities to learn and begin again.

And remember; you're not 'doing' mindfulness – you are *being* mindful. And each time you are mindful, you create small shifts and changes that evolve into who and how you are.

---

### Exercise: Revisit one of the days

Today, choose one of the past 20 days to read again. Choose any of the days to read – do the exercises and carry out the intention for that day.

---

# Begin again

Having read this book, you may want to revisit each of the 21 days. You could of course, begin at Day 1 of this book and work your way through all the days again. But there are several other ways you can revisit each of the days:

- Revisit each of the days in random order.
- Begin with the days that you found most interesting, easy to understand or enjoyable.
- Focus on one specific day of your choosing every two or three days.
- Rather than read through a whole day, just choose a different exercise to do on any one day or every few days.
- Just dip into the book every few weeks.
- Read other mindfulness books or attend mindfulness classes, workshops or retreats.

Just know that mindfulness is not something you 'do' until you have perfected it. Rather, it's a continuous practice; a way of thinking and behaving, doing and being to carry with you.

# Affirmations

- One step at a time.
- The present is always an opportunity to begin again.
- Every day is a new beginning. Take a breath and start again.

# Key points

- Establishing and maintaining new ways of thinking and behaving are more likely to happen if you can accept them as being part of a process; a continual series of gradual changes that will take time to establish.

- It's the regular practice that is key. Even short amounts of time on a 'daily-ish' basis will help you establish a mindfulness practice as a habit.

- Patience and trust are part of the process of establishing and maintaining mindfulness in your life. Be patient with yourself; don't think of relapses in being mindful as failure, instead, think of relapses as part of the process of change; opportunities to learn and begin again.

- **Set yourself an intention:** Today, revisit one of the past 20 days. And from now on, revisit the different days on a daily or 'daily-ish' basis to help remind and encourage you to be mindful.